Kitchen Love Story

A Female Cabinetmaker's Guide to Designing a Kitchen You Will Love

Camille Finan

SparkPress, a BookSparks Imprint
A Division of SparkPoint Studio, LLC

Published by SparkPress, a BookSparks imprint,
A division of SparkPoint Studio, LLC
Tempe, Arizona, USA, 85281
www.sparkpointstudio.com

Printed in the United States of America.

ISBN: 978-1-940716-53-4 (paperback)
ISBN: 978-1-940716-52-7 (ebook)

Cover design © Julie Metz, Ltd./metzdesign.com
Cover photo © Getty Images
Author photo © Jeanie Lapenna, Sweet Jean Photography
Interior design and composition: Maureen Forys, Happenstance Type-O-Rama
Formatting by Polgarus Studio

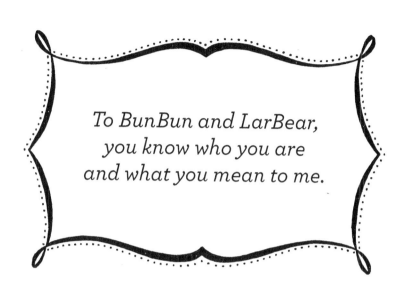

To BunBun and LarBear,
you know who you are
and what you mean to me.

Table of Contents

Introduction

So . . . you want a kitchen that you will love. You imagine awakening to a sunny day. Music plays as you stretch and put on your robe. You waltz down the hallway to your kitchen and breeze through breakfast. Everything you need is at your fingertips, and your smiling family members enjoy the meal you've prepared.

Okay, I know what you're thinking. Right now, you hate your kitchen and you're wondering how on Earth you're going to get from your kitchen nightmare to that dreamlike magical kitchen you love so much that you want to write it a love letter.

I understand where you're coming from. For fifteen years, I've worked with thousands of women who've hated their kitchens.

Not just hate, like you hate the ugly sweater your aunt gave you on your birthday.

I mean *REALLY* hate. . . .

Hate like the-boyfriend-who-cheated-on-you, wrecked-your-car, and slept-with-your-sister hate.

Deep.

Dark.

Revenge worthy.

Hate.

And, you're not alone. Most women I work with think that their kitchen is the worst kitchen ever built. No really. The worst.

And after all of these years helping women fall in love with their kitchens, I also know this. . . .

It's not your kitchen's fault.

Your kitchen isn't bad . . . it's just designed badly.

And I know why.

Your kitchen, like most kitchens being built today, was probably designed by an old-school traditional cabinetmaker, who still thinks that oak is in style and spends more time in his woodshop than actually cooking.

Allow me to introduce myself. My name is Camille Finan and if I was standing in front of you, there's no way you would think of me as a contractor. In fact, at a petite five foot three inches tall, I am constantly asked, how did YOU get started as a cabinetmaker?

Carpentry is in my blood. My family has a lineage of craftsmen that we can trace back to Oslo, Norway. As a child, I grew up on construction sites. My father was a general contractor and brought my sister and me to many job sites in the wild foothills of Northern California. To this day, memories of the ping of a hammer driving a nail into new lumber and the vision of a Schlitz beer can precariously perched on a ladder are fresh—as if they happened yesterday. I loved the freedom, creativity, and the satisfaction my father experienced building beautiful things.

After high school, the lure of the "American Dream" called me to college, an MBA, and successfully starting and running several businesses in other fields. Still, I wasn't happy. None of these successes gave me the deep satisfaction I felt in my younger days, so I decided to leave "traditional work" and get back into carpentry.

I joined the United Brotherhood of Carpenters (the carpenters union) and worked for many years all over California doing all types of finish carpentry. I eventually found my niche in kitchens, learning both cabinets and countertop fabrication.

Here I was, a petite woman working in a man's world: construction—and I loved it. As my work in carpentry continued, I began to see that I had something special to offer. Something that was missing in the market. And so,

I knew it was time. I was ready to open my own business again—this time, doing what I loved most.

As my kitchen remodeling business grew, I became frustrated with the industry, specifically how the industry treats women. I noticed that, almost like the stereotypical car salesmen, most contractors didn't care about how a woman used her kitchen. They were simply trying to sell a remodel and inflate the price as much as possible with "cool and expensive" but useless items. Of course not everyone in the industry is like that, but enough of them are that it has made me realize that the industry has to change. As an insider that builds and installs cabinets and countertops every day, it is my hope that I can eliminate the mystery and pull back the curtain to shed some light on how to remodel your kitchen and turn your kitchen hate into a kitchen love story. I look at a kitchen remodel very differently from most cabinetmakers or contractors. I bring a fresh approach to design and functionality. What makes me, and therefore this book, different? Specifically. . . .

 ## I design from the inside out.

In this book, I'll be sharing with you what I've learned. I'll give you simple instructions for how to manage the remodel of your own kitchen using the ideas and strategies I use with my clients. Together we'll explore the tricks to designing a kitchen that is perfect for *you* and how *you* live. AND I'll show you how to avoid being ripped off.

But first, I have a confession to make. As a woman in a man's industry, I have felt a little like a spy—a counter agent (no pun intended). Let me explain. I have spent those years in the construction industry—listening to women complain about my industry, or more specifically, about old-school, male cabinetmakers and contractors. The truth of the matter is that customers are NOT happy. They are fed up. Maybe you are too.

Women are frustrated—sick and tired of contractors who are not problem solvers. They complain to me about feeling talked down to. Women are annoyed that no one seems to care how she uses her kitchen or how to make it more functional. They hate it when it's considered a waste of time if she wants help with design or figuring out costs.

And it drives women nuts when the only options presented as valid or important are taking out walls and moving the sink and appliances to all new locations. Seriously?

How does that help you figure out where to keep the Ziploc bags?

Basically, old-school contractors wanted to spend the least amount of time possible with these women who became my customers. They wanted to spend zero time being really creative. They just wanted to go on as they always have, designing old-school cabinets.

That's why I created this book. After all of my years in the industry here is what I know from my experience:

- Real families need real solutions to everyday problems. They want honest advice about the scope of work, reasonable prices, realistic schedules, etc.

- Seventy-five percent (75%) of average families who want to remodel their kitchens only have $15,000–$60,000.

- Eighty percent (80%) of average families don't have the funds to move walls, change windows, or shift fundamental items like the sink or stove location.

- Ninty-five percent (95%) of the time, it is too expensive to move the refrigerator to a new location.

- Eighty percent (80%) of average families cannot afford to hire a general contractor (sometimes referred to as a GC). And most of the time, they think it is a waste of money even if they have the funds.

The hard truth is that old-school cabinetmakers are not problem solvers and it's a terrible disservice to the American consumer. It's time for women to be heard. It's time we stop being made to feel like a burden and a hassle. It's time for our industry to:

- Step up, and remember how to provide an excellent consumer experience

- Talk about regular and reasonable approaches to kitchen remodeling

- Discuss the fact that kitchens all share the same contents and have the same basic needs

- Concentrate on common and completely fixable problems that average families face every day

I wrote this book to start a revolution—and to give you hope—because there is another way.

Throughout these pages, I will share a simple plan to actually remodel your kitchen—without moving the walls, the sink, or the stove. You don't have to change any structural items to get a kitchen you will love. ANY kitchen can benefit from the action plan in this book. I will prove to you that the smallest but right changes can make a HUGE impact on how much you enjoy your kitchen.

So let's start off on the same page. If you're reading this book you are as excited as you are overwhelmed by the thought of a kitchen remodel!

 ## And the bottom line is you are probably STUCK.

I think we can all agree that there are almost TOO many choices, TOO many options, and no guide for how to sift through it all.

How do I pick a good cabinet?

How do I figure out the cost of a granite countertop?

How do I figure out what my dream kitchen will look like?

How do I organize all the contractors?

How do I protect myself from lousy workmanship and cost overruns?

How do I make sure my new kitchen is much, much better than my last one?

If these questions are rolling around in your head, this book will answer them and many more. But perhaps the most important question is the one you didn't even know to ask.

WHAT is a kitchen remodel? So many homeowners use the term but don't really have any idea of the context and scale of this type of project. They are unprepared for the journey and how it will impact their lives. We'll begin with an explanation of this. Throughout the book to illustrate my concepts I will use the story of two women, Eva and Elaine, who have very different situations. You will see their stories unfold through each stage of this book. Using their stories as illustrations will provide the framework you need to learn and some stepping stones to build your confidence for your own remodel.

I often hear people discussing a construction project or remodel gone bad and I cringe at some of the stories I hear. A kitchen remodel can be confusing, overwhelming, and just plain frustrating. But it doesn't have to be this way. With the proper support and planning, you can minimize the stress and overwhelming sense of dread.

Think of it like this: let's say your boss comes to you and asks you to plan a huge party. You're honored that he recognizes your talent for planning. However, when he tells you that your budget is $50,000 your heart sinks. You ask some questions and find out that the party is for some very important clients and that the survival of the company depends on the success of this party. He tells you the date for the party is in four months and your heart races! This is a huge responsibility and you struggle with where to start.

Now, would you just call your sister and ask her to bake some cookies and whip up a few appetizers? Would you have your neighbor come and decorate? Would you just ask the first person who submitted a bid to do the food? Or use your neighbor's backyard? Heck no! You would spend hours and hours scouting locations, interviewing vendors, and sampling food. You'd spend more hours on the phone getting bids, checking references, coordinating and stressing over the big day! You might even hire a *party planner* to help with some of the really big stuff.

This is what a kitchen remodel is like. There are dozens of decisions to make, "tons" of research to do, things to learn about, and many things to coordinate. The timing must be impeccable and the quality must shine! And everything has to work within the budget.

Eva & Elaine

To show this process more fully, it's time to meet Eva and Elaine.

Each woman has struggled for years with a kitchen she hates. They are finally ready to take the process seriously and give it the attention it deserves. So let's meet these ladies so we can get to know their individual situations.

Eva is a single mom, recently divorced. She lives in Georgia and has lived in her current house for seven years. She hated the kitchen from the minute she bought the house, but never had the money to redo it. She's been saving for it and thinking about it all those years. She has a folder three inches thick of magazines and torn out pages of ideas she likes. She has $23,500 saved and isn't sure if that will be enough. She doesn't plan to live in this home forever, but she wants to enjoy the kitchen for at least seven years. She really likes beautiful furniture and would love to include some element of that in the new kitchen.

Elaine has been married for sixteen years and has two kids, ages seven and twelve. She lives in California and has a traditional tract home with a big oak kitchen. She's hated it for at least ten years but with kids and expenses, she just couldn't find the time to move forward. She also has a pile of ideas but they are in a shoebox. Her husband finally agreed that this would be the year to finally remodel the kitchen and they have put away $56,000 for the remodel. He loves to cook and would really love a chef-quality Wolf stove but they aren't sure if they can afford it. They've talked to a lot of contractors, but so far, they haven't felt comfortable pulling the trigger. They don't want to get in over their heads. Lastly, they can't seem to agree on the style or color. She would love a pretty white kitchen but he really wants a dark cherry kitchen. They've argued about it for years and no one is budging.

Here's what most kitchens look like—cluttered, disorganized and just plain bad.

All Kitchens Have the Same Qualities

Discovering What's Broken and Why

The kitchen is the center of the home. It's the place where we come together to talk, laugh, cry, vent, enjoy meals, fight, and make up. It is where families have grown up together, parents and kids, trying to make their way through life. Our kitchen can be a place of comfort and fun, inspiration and discovery. Or it can be a chaotic, aggravating source of anxiety and frustration.

Our kitchens are a mirror image of how our families function.

For many years, I have watched how my clients live their lives because I am in their home every day. I have assisted them in bringing the kitchen of their dreams to fruition. I've helped turn pandemonium into peace and harmony on a user-friendly budget. I've learned that all families, regardless of size, have the same basic needs and mostly the same fundamental items in their kitchens. How well (or poorly) the kitchen is designed and organized will either solve problems or intensify them. A well-thought out, but simple and effective design can make a kitchen a delight to work in and a pleasure to be in.

 ## The kitchen is unconcerned with perfection, instead it just wants to enjoy life.

See . . . your kitchen isn't as high maintenance as you think. It just wants you to be able to spontaneously bake a sheet of cookies with your five-year-old daughter who is celebrating a school accomplishment, without the hassle of having to unload an entire cabinet to get to one simple, thin, little cookie sheet.

Wouldn't that be nice?

Your kitchen wants you to sleep quietly and restfully on a rainy Sunday morning without the sound of drawers and doors slamming shut. It longs for you to be able to grab a pot in seconds to boil pasta for Sunday night dinner or to whip something up for the big game without unloading an entire cabinet.

When all these simple demands are met, you can relax and enjoy being in your kitchen. Remember, it's not necessarily about how fancy your kitchen is or trying to impress your neighbor. It's about you and your relationship with your kitchen and how it affects your life and family. These happy-go-lucky kitchens are the types of kitchens that I build and the type of kitchen this book will help you recreate in your own home.

Making it "pretty" is the easy part. Creating a kitchen that combines function, design, and ease of use and that caters to your needs is a little more complicated—but certainly not impossible. As you read on, you'll discover a roadmap that explains in simple terms all of the options that will actually work for your dream kitchen.

Since the clients I work with are primarily women (95% to be exact), I have an an "insider's" perspective to what you want in a kitchen and also what drives you crazy. Through this journey to remodel your kitchen, I'll show you how to avoid the potholes and speed bumps along the way. You'll get a woman's perspective along with an industry expert's wisdom and guidance.

When my father was doing remodels, it was traditionally the husband who dealt with the contractor and made all of the final decisions. These days, women are very involved with the decision-making process, if not running the whole show. This can be a really good thing and a really bad thing. Let me explain why.

It's a good thing because you are emotionally invested in the design. You're open to much more variety which includes different materials and different finishes, and you usually enjoy the process of researching all of the possibilities.

On the downside, it can be counterproductive because you may see an impossible number of options that you love and want. It can be challenging and overwhelming to sort through all of the possibilities without creating a budgetary monster! This book will help you manage your expectations, while still getting the majority of what you want at a reasonable price.

 ## After many years of building kitchens for women, I've developed a list of features that I feel will truly improve your life.

These items are often not the "typical," expensive items that are pushed in the cabinetry industry. Some of them are not flashy and you may barely notice them. They simply work and work beautifully, and are in my opinion, essential to helping your kitchen function the way you want it to.

It's kind of like finally finding that perfect pair of jeans. You know the ones—they fit like they were custom-made just for you and they make your butt look amazing. These features will make your kitchen look and feel amazing. They run the gamut from small, fairly simple details to larger items that function as the workhorse in "your" kitchen, and together, they add up to create a synergy that can be quite dramatic!

So like I said in the introduction, I understand that right now you hate your kitchen and you think it's the worst one ever designed. I am here to tell you that your kitchen is just unloved and misunderstood. Let's start with an inventory and see if any of these sound familiar.

- No handles on the doors and drawers (but there *are* loads of dirty fingerprints).

- Water and food stains all over the surfaces and no amount of "elbow grease" or magical cleaners will get them out.

- "Stuff" crammed into every orifice sometimes falling out onto you when you open a cabinet door.

- You're frequently bending, stooping, reaching to get things out of the cabinets.

- You have to get out a stepstool any time you need anything.

- Cooking usually involves a diving expedition into several cabinets to get that thing in the back that you need.

- Your pantry is loaded with stuff but you can't ever find what you need.

- Getting a container to store leftovers is like a plastic lid scavenger hunt.

- You eat out or use pre-packaged meals often because it takes too long to cook from scratch.

- Only one person can cook in the kitchen at a time because you keep getting in each other's way.

- You have several jars of nutmeg, because you can never find it when you need it.

- The thought of having to host a dinner at your house strikes fear in your heart.

The truth is that this poor kitchen has stopped functioning completely, and your family only uses the kitchen for what they need to "barely" survive. The kitchen just sits there, dirty, dusty, unloved in dark abandonment, waiting to be "used" again, wishing it could see the light of day. If any of this sounds familiar, you are not alone.

Our job is to transform this mess into a lovely design that also functions well for the needs of your family. And I stress "the needs of your family." One thing I've found after working in thousands of kitchens—no matter the size of their budget—is that nearly every family has the same kitchen-related needs. Now don't get me wrong, your family like most others will have some slightly unique factor, but let's tackle the 95% of things that all kitchens have in common first.

Your kitchen will store most, if not all, of the following items:

- Utensils

- Big cooking spoons and spatulas

- Plastic storage bags and aluminum foil

- Dish towels

- Spices

- Cooking oil and sprays

- Pots/pans

- Cookie sheets

- Glass baking dishes

- Tupperware

- Wine/liquor

- Kids' sippy cups and plates

- Big mixing bowls (salad and pasta)

- Roasting pans

- Dinner plates and bowls

- Water glasses

- Wine glasses

- Coffee cups

- Pantry items

    + snacks (chips, crackers, cookies)

    + cereal boxes

    + canned goods

    + drinks

    + baking goods

    + kids' food

As a basic design starting point, all kitchens must have a place for these items. Now you might ask, "But don't cabinetmakers and kitchen designers think about this when building cabinets?" I can tell you unequivocally, **they do not**. And everybody, both the consumer and the builder, assume that all these things will magically find a place in the new kitchen. The problem is that most kitchen cabinetmakers who build for the average family haven't changed their traditional design model. And the design model is broken.

 ## The problem is that kitchen cabinetmakers and builders targeting the average family haven't changed what they do and what they sell all that much.

For the last thirty years there were two basic types of cabinet jobs: budget and custom. Budget cabinets consisted of cheap materials and hardware and were poorly designed. Custom cabinets used the best materials, best finishes, and had the most "premium" features and gadgets, and generally were marked up the most. Custom cabinets are the ones you see currently in all of those magazines you browse.

In the "budget" world, basic cabinet design hasn't changed much, if at all. They are still working off the model wherein families had just basic cooking equipment, plates, cups, and bowls. That is no longer the average reality in the kitchen today. Over the last fifteen years, the advent of TV cooking shows, and even entire television networks devoted to the subject, has dramatically changed the number of items and variety of foods stored in the average kitchen. Yet you will still see the same basic cabinet design that includes doors on base cabinets, drawers that are too small to store items properly, horrible hardware, etc. These old-style budget cabinets create a dysfunctional kitchen that cannot store all the additional food and gear the average modern-day family has accumulated.

In the "custom" world, lots of advances have been made in materials, hardware, and finishes. And the cost of each has fallen dramatically. However, cabinetmakers are still selling the older models. Even though these advances are very affordable now, cabinetmakers rarely offer these features to the average family. In the "custom" world, they are still selling a lot of useless, very expensive gadgets that just don't work well but look exciting. Neither of these approaches solves the problem of where to put your kitchen items for easy accessibility on an affordable budget.

Now you know why your kitchen doesn't work. The contents of your kitchen need to be taken into consideration and stored efficiently to make it functional. That's why I created a new way to design and build a kitchen. I strongly believe in taking the best and most useful "premium" features, that are affordable and actually work, and mixing them with thoughtful design. In other words, *designing your kitchen from the inside out*.

So let's look further into what I mean by design from the inside out (DFIO) and why I think this strategy works better than the old model.

Design From the Inside Out

Discovering What Works!

Like most people, you probably do the same activities in your kitchen during specific times of the day. Likely you are still the primary food purchaser and cook in your home. If you have children, you are typically the one getting the Ramen, fish sticks, and spaghetti together. Even if your partner is the one who is cooking, oftentimes, I still find that you are the one who decides where things get stored.

You decide what goes on the upper shelves, what goes in the pantry, what gets shoved in the back, and what is kept close for ease of use. You're probably the one who obsesses about a new kitchen. You are most likely the one who daydreams about it, collects magazines, and talks to girlfriends about your dream kitchen.

So, when you finally get down to creating your masterpiece, you may try to fit every idea you have ever had into the plan. Unfortunately, all this planning and dreaming never solves any of the "core" problems.

Are you convinced that bigger is always better and if you could only add MORE SPACE, MORE SHELVES, and EVERY GADGET YOU CAN IMAGINE that would be awesome? Right? Wrong.

 ## Adding more space and more cabinets isn't really going to solve the problem, it's what you do with the space that is most crucial.

Designing from the inside out means that we first utilize the existing space and find an *accessible* place to store all your basic kitchen contents by incorporating modern "premium" features found in the best cabinetry. Affordable features that actually work. Most families cannot afford to move walls. When you follow my plan, you'll find that you have plenty of room without wall relocation. It means following a few simple principles to provide a framework for a well-organized kitchen (contents) and well-designed kitchen (features). By designing from the inside out, you will avoid poor organization due to cabinets that aren't designed to fit your needs.

How To Begin Designing From the Inside Out

1. Take an inventory of existing contents

2. Itemize needs and kitchen wish list

3. Determine features that best accommodate your needs

4. Know where your stuff is going to go in the new kitchen

5. Design the "pretty" outside part to include the above-mentioned considerations

So let's start by looking at what's *not* working right now. This will help you decide what you DO want. Let's see if any of these symptoms look familiar to you in your own kitchen.

- Pots and pans stuffed into base cabinet (door), randomly stacked and mixed with big and small pans shoved together in a disorganized manner. Typically, you may have to kneel on the ground to pull much of the contents out onto the floor and then reach all the way to the back for that certain pot you are looking for. Or you abort mission and use an oversized lid instead of the one that fits. Sound familiar?

- Plastic food storage containers are shoved into every spare spot, some in one cabinet, some scattered in a few drawers, while others are in an upper cabinet. Often, lids are separated from the bottoms. Absolutely nothing matches, and there is way too much of it. Frustrating, right?

- Heavy glass baking dishes are stacked high in upper cabinets, and you have to stand on a chair to bring multiple dishes down at once, so you can sort through them to find the one you were originally reaching for.

- Spices of all shapes and sizes are usually in the upper cabinet closest to the stove, drying out from the heat and stuffed in willy-nilly, sometimes with a turntable and sometimes without. Is it basil? Tarragon? Parsley? You have to pull them all out to find what you want.

- The pantry is one of the biggest frustrations in the kitchen for most families. It never starts out that way. Who doesn't love a pantry right? Until it turns into a volcanic eruption of containers tumbling out as you reach for something. Tall cereal boxes end up mixed in with small canned goods, snack bags, chips, baking goods, water bottles, and dessert boxes. Every possible combination of shapes, sizes, and items are jammed in on fixed shelves, which result in many layers stacked on top of each other. Did I just describe your pantry?

- Garbage. It's a dirty word in the kitchen, literally. Dirty and foul-smelling, the garbage is usually placed in a fairly large can next to the island or at the end of the cabinet run. What's worse than cooking something that smells wonderful and then having to throw something away and phew! What's that smell? Sometimes, the overflowing trash can is found crammed under a sink. Any time you need to throw something away, the person doing dishes must stop what they're doing and side step, so that you can gain access. The door gets in the way of your family functioning properly. Annoying, right?

Most of these problems are a result of *dis*organization, because the cabinetry isn't helping you be organized. It's not necessarily because of a lack of space. So the solution is to figure out what kind of cabinetry will allow you to function in the existing space you have.

So what did you find when you did your inventory? Did any of the above qualities surface in your kitchen?

Part of the storage solution is using the following four organizational rules and creating cabinetry features around the items that need to be stowed.

Let's start by sorting out these items.

Step 1: Separate the rarely used from the everyday items

In every kitchen there are things that are used on an everyday basis like small skillets and a pot to make macaroni and cheese. But there are also lots of things you only use once a month or just once a year. These should never be mixed together. For instance, one area should have all of your small skillets that you use often throughout the week, and your large rarely used cast iron and huge pots should be stored in another place.

Step 2: Separate the lightweight from the heavyweight

It might seem to make sense to slip a lightweight cookie sheet underneath heavy roasting pans or pots, but this makes the cookie sheets basically unreachable. As another example, I've even seen a huge heavy spaghetti pot mixed in with small little bowls. These should not be stored together. So we need to find a place for the cookie sheet that is accessible and not mixed in with heavy items.

Eva & Elaine

Eva: After doing an inventory of her existing kitchen, Eva found that, since she doesn't have a pantry, she is currently using one of her upper cabinets to store all her dry goods and canned goods. Her chips are stuffed into a bottom cabinet. Her dishtowels are crammed into a tiny little drawer that never shuts. All of her pots and pans are sitting in base cabinets with doors and something tumbles out every time she needs to cook. Additionally, she has a cabinet with a lazy susan that is dark and has all her big salad bowls crammed into it. It has a really small opening that barely allows the bowls to squeeze through. Her biggest frustration is that she doesn't have enough room to store spices and cooking essentials because her upper cabinets are full of plates, cups, and canned goods.

Elaine: While she feels fortunate that her husband loves to cook, her biggest complaint is the huge number of pots and pans stacked to the brim in her base cabinet with doors. Every time she wants to use one pan she has to unload the entire cabinet. In her inventory, Elaine noticed that she had multiple boxes of old outdated pastas and cereal crammed all the way to the back of her existing pantry. She found Tupperware in there too, along with old canned goods. All of her spices were in an upper cabinet, making it impossible to store wine glasses where they are supposed to go. Her garbage was a stinking mess, with the puppy always tipping it over. She found it frustrating to look for her special gourmet gadget. She could never find it because it was buried in one huge drawer that was filled to the brim. She really hated to use her kitchen these days because it was such an effort.

Can you relate to Eva or Elaine's predicament? Let's talk about figuring out how to solve the space problem.

Step 3: Separate the smalls from the talls

When you mix small tea boxes and canned goods with tall cereal boxes everything naturally gets disorganized. This leads to a huge waste of space.

Step 4: Follow the ten-inch rule

Everyone I meet thinks they "use" their cabinets. An average base cabinet unit is twenty-four inches deep and is filled to the brim. However, in my experience, most people only really use the first ten inches of their kitchen cabinets. Why? Because that's the space you can see. It's where the light falls when you open the door in a base cabinet. Most people have the false impression that they are truly "using" all the space in their cabinets. What actually happens is that they cram stuff into every nook and cranny. They look for a place to put something and back it goes into the deep dark depths of the cabinet. Then they have to unload the entire cabinet to get that one thing out.

Because it's so much trouble to get that item out of the cabinet, they change their behavior over a period of time. As a result they only "use" a small percentage of the items they actually own. Mostly they just store stuff and have no idea what they actually need. When I do a remodel, my goal is to build cabinets that allow the homeowner to actually use the full twenty-four inch depth of base cabinets and the full twelve inches of a standard upper cabinet.

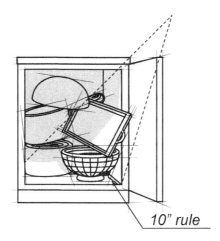

10" rule

If we imagine reorganizing our new kitchen using these guiding principles, we need cabinetry features that will allow us to maintain this organization. In the next section, I will explore each feature and how it solves the most common problems in kitchens today. These are the same features that are often sold as "premium" and are often touted as very expensive upgrades. To me, they are the only solution to the problems listed above. They are not as expensive as you may have been led to believe, and they are worth every penny!

Here's what we want your dream kitchen to look like.

Nine Features of a Good Kitchen

Moving Forward: Let's See What Will Work for You

Now that you understand designing from the inside out (DFIO) and why it's so important in a kitchen, let's talk about the best and most cost-effective ways to solve the common design flaws in your kitchen.

As far as the concept and actual designing of your kitchen, if you're like most people, so far your research has gone something like this:

1. Buy a bunch of kitchen design magazines,

2. Talk to a multitude of friends,

3. Look at hundreds or thousands (yikes!) of pictures,

4. Think about it, for months or even years . . . but nothing moves forward. "

Learn more at *www.divinekitchen.net/good_features.*

You're overwhelmed with options and choices with a myriad of varying visual images. You're worried that your kitchen will never look like the ones in the fancy magazines and you're completely and utterly . . . stuck.

No, I am not a mind reader. This is typically the state of mind my clients are in when I'm asked to bid on a job. By the time I get referred by a close friend or neighbor, frustrations and anxiety are palpable, and I'm the only salvation. In fact, at this point expectations are so high that I can't possibly meet them. So, out of necessity, I've developed a simple, effective system that translates what is in all of those magazines, both visually and functionally.

But before I share my system, you need to understand that no kitchen can be everything to everyone all at once. It's simply impossible! Your kitchen, like every kitchen I've worked on, is limited by some sort of constraint—like overall size, the length of the walls for cabinet installation, where appliances can be located, and of course, money. Never fear! Even within those fixed constraints, there is plenty of room for improvement.

So let's get started with my "Nine Features of a Great Kitchen." This list was created just for you—the "regular woman" who doesn't have the budget for a kitchen designer and who isn't hiring an architect to design your kitchen. These features are for any budget, no matter its size, and apply across every design style. They will help make your kitchen work FOR you, affordably.

Feature No. 1: Keep Your Cabinets Quiet

 One of the most irritating disturbances on a Sunday morning is hearing kitchen doors slam as you are trying to sleep in!

Am I right? This is something that irks many people, and I happen to agree. I am cringing just thinking about it. Truly, this is the number-one complaint that I get when bidding on a job; people hate how loud those cabinet doors are when they are being used.

Honestly, this is one of the easiest issues to fix! For years in the cabinet industry, it has been touted and sold as a huge upgrade to use soft-closing hinges. But for me, it is a no-brainer. In fact, I refuse to sell a job now without soft-closing European-style hinges. This style of hinge is not visible when the cabinet door is closed.

Soft-closing hinges incorporate a tiny, little mechanism in the hinge that prevents the door from slamming shut. Simple, right? That's what I think too. Anyone who tells you it's a big, expensive thing is being less than honest.

My absolute favorite brand is the top-of-the-line manufacturer Blum. I wouldn't go with any other company; they're the best. Don't let someone talk you into some cheap alternative; it simply won't work as well.

Example: If you have 12 cabinet doors, this would equal 24 soft-closing hinges. Each hinge costs $8.50. Your total for hinges is $204.

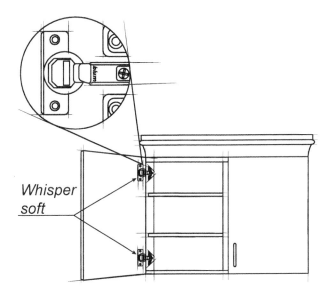

Whisper soft

Not only will it reduce kitchen noise dramatically and save so much aggravation, but it will also save your doors by ultimately preventing constant wood on wood slamming. WIN-WIN!

Feature No. 2: Drawers You Can Bank On

The most important change you can make when redesigning your new kitchen cabinets is to install as many drawer units on the bottom cabinets as possible instead of installing cabinets with doors.

I know it may seem odd to have mostly drawers in the base cabinets, but trust me, it is the single biggest change you can make and it will dramatically transform your kitchen and the way you use it!

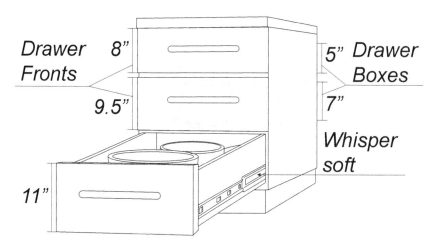

For years high-end designers have been using this feature in very expensive kitchens, but it's not a cost-prohibitive feature! The benefits far outweigh the investment. Here's why:

1. Remember the ten-inch rule? Because drawers slide out and you look down into them, you can see all your items clearly and reach all your items quickly. Imagine looking straight down into a cabinet instead of only being able to view items from the front. Remember, your drawers extend fully using Blum slides, so you can see literally every inch of space within that drawer in a single glance.

2. Rather than a single open space, drawers make it is easier to separate and organize different types of items. In a traditional base cabinet, you have to stack pots and pans inside of each other, and in front of each other, in order to use all of the space. In a fully extended drawer,

you'll still stack some of your pots, but you also have three distinct drawers to organize within instead of a single cabinet.

In cabinets with doors, everything stacks on top of each other. You have to take everything out of the cabinet just to get one pot. After doing that a dozen times, you'll probably change your behavior: you'll stack less so you can see what's in there or you'll only put stuff in there that you rarely use. You'll keep commonly used items in a more accessible location and will end up not using the other items at all.

Benefits of Base Drawers not Doors

- Able to see contents because you are looking down instead of having to bend over and look back in

- Can access ALL the volume

- Can pull the middle drawer out and get to its contents easily

- Can avoid having to take things in and out to get something from the back

- Allows you to store tallest things in the bottom drawer, which are now not interacting with things in the middle, and those aren't messing with the things in the top 5″ drawer box

- Minimizes disruption

3. Because the top drawer is tall enough to place all your smaller items, it frees up the middle and bottom drawers for all the "workhorse" items you use everyday (like spaghetti pots, frying pans, and sauce pans). But you'll treat these drawers differently than you treat your traditional base cabinets. If you use small tools like your cheese grater and measuring cups frequently, you'll be able to place these in the drawers as well for easy access. Remember, DFIO is all about efficiency!

Want to see exactly how I organize these base cabinet drawers? Download the free Organization Chart at *www.divinekitchen.net/ organization-chart*.

Nothing changes the *feel* of a kitchen like installing modern drawers. Instead of just shoving stuff in cabinets randomly and never being able to remember where it all is, you will easily be able to create a storage system and access it anytime.

And I know what you are thinking—if my kitchen was *bigger* of course I would install more drawer units. But actually **the smaller the kitchen, the MORE important they are**.

Traditional kitchens make you stack all your stuff, but even if you stack it as much as you can, you still aren't actually using the full volume of the base cabinet and you certainly aren't seeing all your stuff.

Being able to *see* and *grab* your stuff easily without unloading the entire cabinet means you will no longer change your behavior to stop using things that are too difficult to get to quickly. My goal is to prevent you from changing your kitchen behavior because you can't easily get to items in the base cabinets.

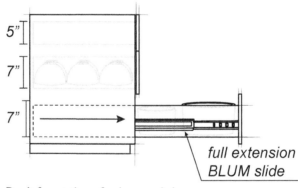

5"
7"
7"

full extension BLUM slide

Don't forget the soft-close tracks!

Size Matters

I hope I have convinced you to include this feature in your new kitchen design, but before we move on I just want to make sure you understand the importance of the actual size of this cabinet. Just installing any drawer unit will not work.

💙 *No more digging in dark spaces and rummaging through cabinets to get one specific pan.*

Traditional cabinetmakers have been using the same or similar dimensions for the last 50 to 60 years, making almost no changes to cabinet design. There is so much inefficiency with this model! Believe me, you'll fall in love with your drawers, but you **must** follow these dimensions.

The box: The drawer box is the actual box you place all your stuff in. It needs to be sturdy and tall enough to hold everything. But perhaps the most important part is the top drawer box. Traditional cabinetmakers have always made a three- to four-inch tall drawer box, the smaller the better since it saved wood right? But this size of drawer has been too small for decades. So I started making our drawer boxes five inches tall and *voilà*! All kinds of things now fit in the top drawers. Now all the utensils, spices, Ziploc bags, and tinfoil can fit in the top drawers. By putting the most essential things in the top drawer you free up space for the middle and bottom drawers which are the deepest. Because five-inch top drawers are not standard, remember to specifically ask your cabinetmaker for the deeper drawer!

The slides: Traditional cabinets have cheap plastic rollers, or ball-bearing slides if you are lucky. They only extend three quarters of the way out, making it impossible to actually use the full volume of the drawer box. But for years there has been a better alternative: soft-closing, full-extension slides made by Blum. These are critical because if the slides are not high quality enough, it will be a struggle to pull out big, deep drawers that are filled to the brim. Only Blum makes a slide that will bear the extra weight, fully extend, glide easily in and out, and soft close so they don't bang shut.

The fronts: The drawer front is the pretty part you see and is where the handle is attached. It needs to be larger than the drawer box to cover the face of the cabinet. Because we are doing larger drawer boxes, the front and handle needs to be bigger too. Usually a six- to eight-inch drawer pull (handle) works best.

If you follow these guidelines, your base drawer units will now be able to hold an enormous amount of stuff, much of it heavy pots and pans, glassware, etc. . . . But because the drawers are big enough, have high-quality slides, and have large enough handles, you will easily be able to access much more than you ever thought possible.

Feature No. 3: Spice-Drawer Dreams

I must say this is probably my absolute favorite upgrade! It is so inexpensive and easy to do, and it makes an instant transformation. I'm talking about installing a spice-drawer insert into one of the top drawers. It slides into any top drawer, and is basically a premade maple mini-shelf that allows all of your spices to lie on their backs at a slight angle so you can see (and reach) all of them easily.

How cool is that? Because the spices are laid on their side at a slight angle, you can easily see them and quickly pick what you want. No more searching frantically for the smoked paprika or buying multiple nutmegs because every time you go to cook a new recipe, you think that you're out. Those frustrating days are over!

The insert we use comes thirty inches wide, and we cut it to fit into whatever size drawer you need. It typically costs about $50. Almost every family's spices (the ones you actually use) will fit into this one drawer . . . all within reach, completely and easily accessible, as well as visible.

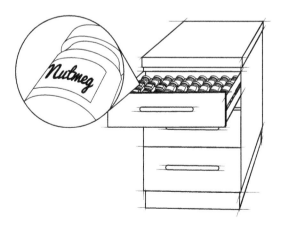

The benefits of this are twofold. Not only does it allow your spices to be beautifully laid out, **all of them visible and accessible at one time** but . . . now you can use the upper cabinet for what it was intended, which is to hold your glasses and coffee mugs.

 Oftentimes I see spices taking up huge amounts of space in an upper cabinet. Spice drawers solve this problem easily AND cost-effectively.

Feature No. 4: Fall In Love With Your Garbage

Yes, I said it. Fall in love with your garbage.

How we, as women, hate our garbage cans. Am I right? They are usually either crammed under the sink, hard to see, or filled to the brim with a God-awful, stinky mess. Either that OR they are in everyone's way at the end of the countertop, next to the island. No matter where it is placed, "the can" always seems to be in the way or completely inaccessible. It doesn't have to be like this anymore!

My favorite way to tackle the "can issue" is to install a simple yet extremely effective garbage can pullout drawer. From the front it looks like a regular base cabinet with a door, but inside it's really a soft-closing garbage can. The construction is fairly simple and doesn't take up much room.

The garbage pullout drawer I recommend is the one I use all of the time, which fits into a twenty-three inch wide base cabinet. I prefer to use a pre-made maple dual can (side-by-side) pullout with can liners in the back. The maple makes it bright and easy to clean. It attaches to a door and slides out easily using a large pull. Then, because it is on soft-closing slides, it slides effortlessly back in place.

To position it, I always try to arrange it, if possible, within a couple of feet of the sink but not right next to it. This way, the person who is washing dishes and using the dishwasher is not affected by the other family members throwing away their trash. Alternatively you can put this drawer unit on a corner of an island, but you must keep in mind how it will be used when pulled out and whether or not it will block traffic.

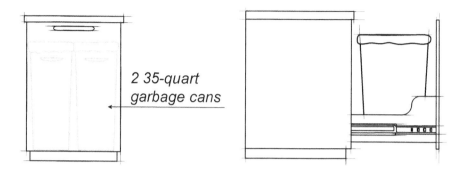

2 35-quart garbage cans

 Dedicated trash cabinets free up another common "pinch point," thus further reducing stress and conflict within families!

 # Feature No. 5: A Pantry That Fits

Cabinetmakers have programmed homeowners to think that they need a HUGE pantry to have a "real kitchen." Don't get me wrong. If you have seven kids and shop every three days to keep their bellies full, you just may need an oversized pantry. However, this is not the typical household.

What I usually run into, even in larger families, is massive amounts of overstocked food jammed into dark shelves, with only 20% of the space actually being utilized. There's just no denying this; I see it all of the time.

Even with all of the obvious (to me) wasted space, pantries are where I run into the most conflict. Explaining to my clients that they actually don't need a gigantic storage space is a hard sell. The truth is that a modest space used wisely, is much more convenient. This is particularly true when you use the other features I've mentioned (a bank of drawers, for example) to maximize space in the remaining cabinets. When you see that you're throwing away fewer expired food items and finding what you do need much more quickly, I am sure you'll agree.

> 💜 *What most families need is a place to put sundries that get used on a daily basis and are frequently stocked and turned over within arms' reach.*

It's time for a new pantry cabinet. This simple, yet extremely effective cabinet is something I personally designed to solve the "pantry cave problem." It is basically a floor-to-ceiling cabinet which easily fits into a twenty-four inch (wide and deep) opening. It contains one or two big drawers on the bottom, usually used for plastic storage containers and lids. The pantry opening spans from your knees to your shoulders. The knees-to-shoulder space is what you would naturally use without stooping, reaching, or stepstools.

Above that are two small doors that can be used to hold tall liquor bottles on one side and infrequently used items such as holiday dishes and pots.

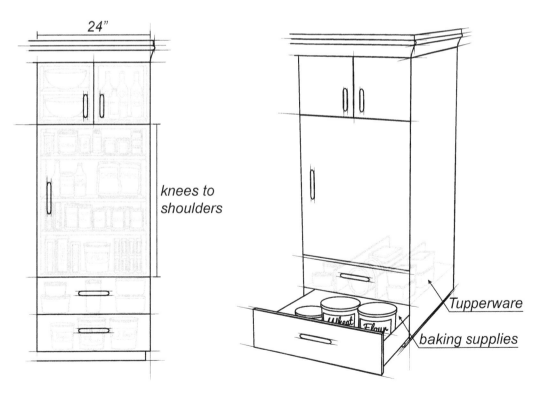

24"

knees to
shoulders

Tupperware

baking supplies

Knees to shoulders, no reaching!

In the main or "pantry" section are two to three prefinished adjustable shelves.

Get ready . . . now comes the fun part!

Because I only use prefinished maple cabinet plywood shelves that are light and bright, items easily slide around. Now it's a breeze to move things around so you can see items in the back of the cabinet.

I organize the cabinet by separating tall, lightweight items which include: cereals, snacks, crackers, and baking boxes, into the tallest portion.

Next, we move on to the canned goods. These should be stored together so when you are looking for a can of tomato soup, you know just where to look.

Last comes odd-shaped items that will fill in other spaces. Remember, because you will not have spices, plastic food containers, zip top bags, or liquor in this space; you will now have free space for the items your family uses on a daily or weekly basis.

If you're still feeling skeptical, stick with me. I know it might be a radical change or sound too simple to be true. This works because of a combination of key elements.

- **Body position:** Because it is specifically built to stock only from the knees to the shoulders, you can see almost everything at once or with just a slight bend. Remember, if you can't see it, you will not be using it regularly.

- **Adjustable shelves:** This is critical to customize the cabinet for the items *your* family actually uses. You can have as many shelves as you need to separate different kinds of items, so a minimal number of things end up in the back.

- **Slippery surface:** Prefinished maple plywood shelves are really smooth and help items slide around. This makes it effortless to pull items in and out or easily slide things out of the way to see other items. Being able to do this feels fantastic. No more dragging or having to pick up cans, jars, or boxes just to put an item in its place; those frustrating days are over!

A special note for bakers: if you love to bake and as a result, have lots of baking supplies, I typically recommend placing those baking supplies in a single large drawer right under the main pantry cabinet. Heavy items, like flour and sugar, should be placed down low in an easy-to-see-and-reach drawer. If left in the main pantry, overcrowding will occur.

Feature No. 6: Tupperware Heaven

Finally, we come to the subject of those plastic storage containers. It's a love-hate relationship. You love them because they're great for storing leftovers and kid's stuff, and you hate them because they just never, ever seem to stay in one place. It's like that awkward pair of shoes you keep meaning to wear, but they never quite seem to work. My solution to this dilemma is to give plastic storage containers a permanent home of their own.

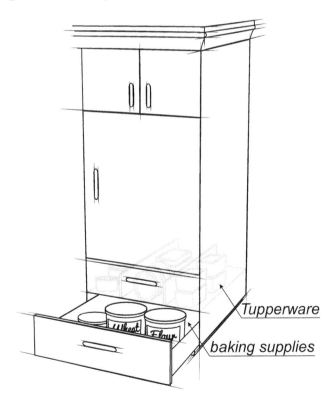

My favorite place to put Tupperware is under the same pantry cabinet that holds essential, daily food items. Either two smaller drawers or better yet, one large drawer is ideal for holding items like these. It is a large and deep drawer that we can easily put dividers in to hold Tupperware and keep it in its place. My preference is to store "matching" Tupperware on the left and then a divider to hold the lids and then one more divider to hold oddly sized items by themselves.

Again, by placing Tupperware in just this one area, you can keep it neat, organized, AND accessible. It sounds like a dream come true, right? In addition, now that you have freed up more space, you have room for something else to go in the main cabinets. It also makes what you have easily visible. No more digging around for matching lids and tubs.

Feature No. 7: Sweet Cookie Sheet Storage

Cookie sheets usually get shoved underneath other items. It's always a hassle to pull everything out from on top just to bake cookies.

So, here's how we separate them from those larger and heavier items: a small base cabinet door, usually about a foot wide. We then put one or two slim dividers inside the floor of the cabinet, so that sheets can "lean" against them. This makes it so much easier to slide a single cookie sheet in and out.

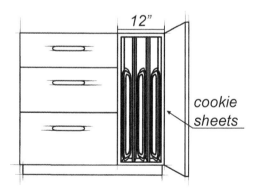

This goes back to my philosophy of separating items you use frequently from items that are occasionally or rarely used. Cookie sheets are typically used frequently for pizzas, fish sticks, quick roasting of veggies, and of course, everyone's favorite, cookies! With all of the various uses for a cookie sheet, you want to be able to quickly and easily slide one out without having to move other items.

💜 *Now you can bake delicious cookies at the drop of a hat!*

Feature No. 8: Handles Like Jewelry

I love jewelry! What woman doesn't? I like to think of handles for your cabinets as jewelry for your custom-made kitchen. I've seen women get almost as excited picking out handles as they do buying that gorgeous new necklace. It's that finishing touch that says "this kitchen is special and loved." If you're like me, you could spend hours poring over hundreds of handle examples.

Now, not to rain on your parade or anything, but it is important to remember that your gorgeous new kitchen adornments need to be chosen not just for looks, but also for function. I strongly recommend, no, *I insist* on pulls that are large enough to get your hand around without your hand touching the cabinet.

What I often find is that the homeowner chooses something that is too dainty. Cute or pretty isn't really workable in a functioning kitchen. See, what happens is, within two months there are food, oils, enzymes, and acids eating into the finish of the cabinets. The longer the gunk is present, the worse it becomes.

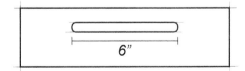

When you've designed your kitchen around large, soft-closing pullout drawers, you will also need a pull that is proportionate to the size of the drawer front. I almost always use a pull six inches or larger.

Please don't even think about buying four inch pulls (which is what ninety percent of big box home improvement stores' inventory consists of.) A four inch pull will literally leave about one-half an inch of space behind the pull in which to shove your hand. This means that the tops of the drawers will get fingernail chips, grime, and food all over them. Think about it. That pretty makes much makes the pull *completely useless.*

 Most people don't realize that your hands should never touch your kitchen cabinets.

Here's why. Think of the fancy furniture you may have in your house. You would never in your wildest dreams walk over to it and use the small, dainty pulls with butter or sauce on your hands and smear it all over the fine finish, would you? Of course not! Obviously, if you and your whole household did this every day, your beautiful furniture and antiques would be destroyed in a matter of months. Even though your kitchen cabinets should have a stronger finish on them, nothing is impervious.

So, when you're picking the style . . . choose pulls from a company that offers several lengths (from five to eight inches long) so that you can use a proportional length on all of your drawers. In fact, be like me. Insist on it. Then your drawers will be the most-used cabinets in your kitchen because you L-O-V-E them and they're actually functional.

Feature No. 9: Refrigerator Cabinet

Last, but certainly not least, let's consider a refrigerator cabinet. If you can afford the space and money to build a custom refrigerator cabinet that is the correct depth—so that you can easily reach the door handles—then by all means, do so! This is the last feature to incorporate into your kitchen design, if you can. Not only does it look beautiful and make the refrigerator blend into the design, if built correctly, it also creates a great deal of extra long-term storage. It is also a great place to store tall or bulky items.

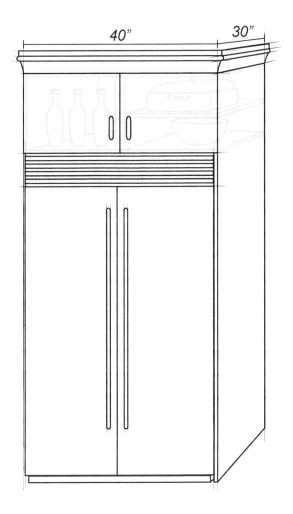

A traditional refrigerator cabinet (over the top) is only about twelve inches deep and is completely inaccessible once the refrigerator is installed. This is because the average women can't reach the door when they are set so far back. I believe there is no reason to install a refrigerator cabinet unless it's at least twenty-four inches deep, if not more. A woman of average height should be able to reach the front of the cabinet without a problem.

A refrigerator cabinet can be used for wine and liquor that are not used often. Many families have numerous bottles crammed into areas that are better suited for items used on a daily basis, so I find that storing them in a refrigerator cabinet works very well. It's easy to see and reach, but not used every day. My clients also use the space in the refrigerator cabinet for storing big roasting pans, holiday dishes, crock pots, all kinds of things not used every day but visible and accessible when needed. It truly comes in handy.

I've given you a lot to think about and hopefully you can see how these features solve some of the most common kitchen problems, without even addressing how it might look on the outside. Both Eva and Elaine are surprised to see that these nine features are viable options.

Eva & Elaine

Eva: "I'd heard about soft-closing hinges because a friend told me about hers. But her kitchen was really expensive, so I figured that was way out of my budget. And I've seen the large pot and pan drawers too, but I never really thought about how useful they would be. I didn't think we could create custom sizes so every drawer is maximized. How wonderful that would be in a small kitchen like mine. The pantry concept really blew me away. I always thought a pantry had to be a huge space to be useful and with my small space I thought it would never work. Now I'm reconsidering it for my plan."

Elaine: "I just never thought about drawers for pots and pans. I'm rethinking my whole layout now. I think adding several banks of drawers would mean we could store other big items as well. I never heard of full extension, and absolutely hate the three-quarter extension slides we have now. I guess I thought all drawers were the same, it never occurred to me there was something so much better. And I'm excited about the soft-closing hinges and spice insert. I love the thought of seeing all my spices at once! My only concern is the refrigerator cabinet. I'm just not sure if it's worth the money. I really want to get the Wolf stove, so I'll have to see if we can afford it."

Features You Do Not Want
Things To Avoid That Are Expensive and Useless

In the last chapter I described the features that I believe are important in functional kitchen cabinets. There may have been a few you hadn't considered. I wanted to take a moment to discuss some of the things you don't want (but maybe think that you do).

These fall into two categories: older design features that create problems, and expensive but useless features that are typically sold through cabinet shops. This is important because, as you go through magazines and talk to your friends, you will probably run into ideas that have a large "wow" factor. They look like a good idea, but in reality, they are expensive without adding very much functionality.

For pictures of things we don't want, go to *www.divinekitchen.net/do-not-want*.

Overrated Features

After surveying hundreds of clients to find out how they actually used the items we installed, I discovered that, of the women who decided to go ahead and install some of these wow-factor items, only a tiny percentage—and I mean one or two people total, were glad they spent the money to do it.

First let's cover the wow-factor items that I believe don't deliver.

Corner Cabinets with Lazy Susans

I hear it all of the time. You want to use every inch of space and so you can't stand the thought of losing that space in the corner. So of course cabinet shops sell lazy susans like they are going out of style. In my experience, this is the most *sold* item but the least *used* item.

Here's the problem: instead of worrying about the one percent of space you are not using in the corner, you should be worrying about the ninety-nine percent that is horribly designed and not used at all. Lazy susan's don't work in most situations for a variety of reasons. It doesn't matter how large the inside portion is, you are limited by the front opening, which is usually quite small.

On top of that, because the opening is small, the cabinet is dark and you can't see any of your stuff. Which means you won't use it. It just sits there. My experience is that they are by far the least useful gadget that has been pushed in the last twenty years. Add on to that the "premium" charge to build it, and it just doesn't deliver. You can easily design a kitchen that has a place for all of your stuff. Your kitchen items will be visible and accessible—and for a lower price. Why waste your money?

Spice-Rack Pullout

This little gadget is sold as an upgrade but has its limitations in application. Once your spices are in the rack you can't actually see them all at once, so you are rooting around, having to kneel on the ground. It won't take long before you stop using it for everyday cooking. Add to that the space it takes up in the cabinets and it's just not worth it. Especially when it is easily replaced by much cheaper and functional spice-drawer insert that fits into an existing drawer box.

Olive-Oil Pullout

This is much like the spice-rack pullout but with the added mess of dripping oil on the floor and sides of the unit. Because you can't see your oils, you have to remove and sort through them to find what you are looking for.

Pantry Pullout

This expensive unit is both cost-prohibitive and cumbersome. The unit itself is very heavy and usually does not slide out easily. This awkwardness gets worse once it is loaded down with canned goods and other heavy items. On top of the cost and dysfunctional nature, once filled, it is hard to locate items because you are trying to find items *from both sides*, making it difficult to create a consistently organized pantry.

Forty-Five Degree Corner Cabinets

Although forty-five degree corner cabinets are pretty and I've done them many times, they do use up a lot of cabinetry wall. I feel that they are an expensive upgrade with very little benefit. If you are doing it for the look and really want them it makes sense, but often I find clients think they are also more efficient, which they are not.

Mixing Bowl/Kitchen Aid Helper

This is an expensive item that lifts or helps your heavy mixer move out of the cabinet on an extended arm/shelf to countertop height. Unfortunately, the actual practical use is just not there. What ends up happening is that you just put the mixer on the countertop anyway because if you actually use the mixer on the extended arm/shelf, food and flour ends up all over your floor. A simple, cost-free solution is to install the adjustable shelf where you will store your mixer at a higher level, so that it is easy to reach inside the cabinet without bending. Then you simply put it on the countertop when you want to use it. Easier cleanup and lighter on the wallet.

Having discussed the overpromoted wow-factor items, we move on to the outdated features that create problems.

Outdated, Old-Style Cabinet Features

Many kitchens feature outdated cabinet features that are sold as great additions to any kitchen design. After all, who wouldn't love more storage and fancy shelves? If those features don't actually work for your kitchen, they're definitely not worth it!

Corner Cabinets with Lazy Susans

Yes, I know. I said it before, but I've listed it twice to show just how much I don't like relying on this feature. If you have to rely on a lazy susan, it just means that the rest of the kitchen is probably not designed well. It should be your absolute last resort.

Fancy Pullout Shelves behind Doors

This is a common feature on older-style cabinets but not as effective as more modern soft-closing drawers. The downside to using a pullout shelf is that you must open all of the doors to pull out the shelf, creating a traffic jam. In addition, the backs of the doors get gouged from shelves hitting them. Finally, they use up a lot of space that could be better used by just installing a drawer box unit. This feature is commonly sold by old-time cabinetmakers that do not want to change and have yet to adapt to modern cabinetry and soft-closing drawers.

Garbage-Can Pullouts under Sink

This is another common feature I see in poorly designed kitchens from older-style cabinetmakers. It costs almost the same amount to install a soft-closing, full-extension cabinet for a pair of thirty-five quart garbage pails. The inferior under-sink pullout, creates a traffic jam around the sink. Other problems include having to move out of the way to use the can, its very limited size, and garbage falling out all over the inside of your cabinets and food getting on the inside of your cabinet door. Yuck!

Center Stiles

This is when a cabinetmaker adds a piece of wood down the middle of the cabinet opening for face-frame cabinets. This older style of building cabinets was the standard for a long time. Unfortunately it is often added in cabinets that don't need the extra strength. With modern cabinet doors that meet next to each other, you don't need the filler between doors. This feature creates a real obstacle to using your cabinets and severely limits the space. I would never suggest purchasing cabinets with center stiles unless it was needed for strength and there were generous openings.

Small Handles and Pulls

This common trait leads to lots of problems on old cabinets and it's a shame when I see that same trait applied to brand new cabinets. No matter what the manufacturer tells you about how strong and protective their finish is, the truth is there is no finish that is impervious to human beings. With small handles and pulls you will be forced to touch your cabinets. Sticky, grimy, gummy hands covered with acidic food and juices will always create damage.

Always use a handle or pull that is generous and will actually fit your hand. This one, very "cheap" feature will do more to save your cabinets than anything else you can do to protect them.

No Handles (a.k.a. the Naked Door)

See above. I would never, ever, *ever* install cabinets without adequate handles and pulls. I would consider it an absolute crime to give my customers the impression that it was okay, knowing the damage that will happen with normal use. It is very common to see doors on older cabinets without handles, and you will see the damage all over them! But I also see this trend in brand new cabinets and it makes my heart hurt. It is done for the some design reasons and also laziness on the part of the contractor. Unless they are laminate (plastic) cabinets, the industry does a huge disservice to customers by not adequately informing them of the damage that *will* occur.

Fixed Shelves

This feature is common in older-style cabinets and seems like such a no-brainer and yet I still see cabinets being sold and installed today with this (non)feature. All shelves should be adjustable to allow for flexibility within each cabinet. You will have tall items and short items, so you will need to be able to adjust the height of the shelves. Please make sure any new cabinets you order only have adjustable shelving. This is mandatory.

So far, we've looked at what I feel are the features you should and should not include in your DFIO layout and hopefully you know what makes sense for your kitchen and why. Now it's time to move into the fun part—designing.

Eva & Elaine

Eva and Elaine are moving right along and are excited to start this next section too.

But both admit that they don't know the first thing about how to design what their dream kitchens will look like. They are anxious and both feel they will never get it "right." There are just too many options! This is a common complaint I get from clients. Most people have a hard time visualizing their design, so I find the following concepts to be helpful. We will use these stepping stones to make sure you feel confident in your choices at each step.

Designing Your Dream Kitchen

Finally . . . We Get to the Fun Part!

Now that we've looked at the insides and organization of the kitchen, it's time to see how it will look on the outside. Even though our focus has been on what's inside the kitchen cabinets, the outsides are just as important in creating a kitchen you'll truly fall in love with. It's possible to have a gorgeous, magazine-worthy kitchen that also works incredibly well in your home. This next section gets down to the nitty-gritty and will start to show you how I design a kitchen using DFIO. I will also show you how I incorporate the colors and materials my clients want.

In order to do that, I will be walking you through three steps—visualizing, dealing with constraints, and laying out a draft plan. By going through each step you will feel more confident about your plan. So remember, this is a marathon, not a sprint. Take your time, absorb the information, and have fun playing with your ideas. Your dream kitchen waits just around the corner.

Visualizing with a Storyboard

It can be really hard to imagine what your new finished kitchen will look like. In the beginning most clients are obsessed with the door style and color of the cabinets. The next concern would probably be the countertop color and type, and then maybe the floor. All three make up the majority of the overall look and style of the kitchen. So the very first step I take when I'm trying to figure out the look of a new kitchen is to make a storyboard, and at a bare minimum have these three items on it.

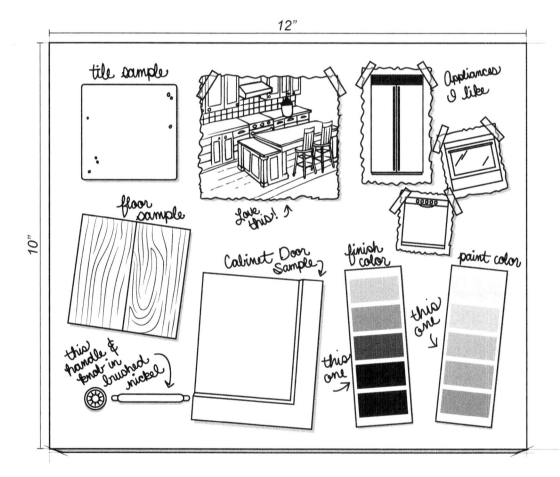

What's a storyboard? Well, it's a physical manifestation of all those ideas running around in your head. It seems obvious to me yet most people don't do it. Professionals always use storyboards to experiment with ideas and see what works. It is quick and inexpensive, and really helps get you started by taking the ideas out of your head and putting them onto something tangible.

Here are the basic steps.

1. Cut out a piece of thick cardboard or white foam board. I like to use a size that is twelve inches wide by ten inches tall. It's lightweight and easy to carry around with you, take to the store, prop up against the back wall of an existing space, etc. But it is also big enough to be sturdy without being awkward. Skip the poster board—it's too big and flimsy to be effective.

2. Rip out pages from magazines, collect paint swatches, tile, cabinet door and finish samples, handles, flooring, and anything else you feel drawn to.

3. Now look at all those items and pictures for a few days. Keep sorting through them refining your preferences. Let it marinate. Once you think you are getting close, start cutting out your favorite magazine or catalog images. Include specific details or finishes. Once you have a pile of stuff that you adore, move on to step 4.

4. Using a hot glue gun, glue those images, tile pieces, paint samples, and wood finishes directly onto the board. I like to drill through the board and attach real handles or knob samples. You can use these to carry the board around from store to store. Remember, if you've attached a handle to your board and you can't get your hand through it, the handle is too small.

5. Now, using your storyboard, you can visit more places, take it to vendors to show them what you are looking for, get quotes, and shop for additional accessories. This more tangible version of the dream kitchen you've imagined allows you to really see if you love your choices. It enables you to visualize numerous features together, in

combination. And it forces you to dispose of options that don't suit the overall scheme.

You can prop up your storyboard in your existing space, look at it in the morning and evening light, and use it to pick out additional samples. Finally, if you decide you like something better, you can substitute the new thing you like and remove the old one.

It may feel like an overly elaborate way to determine the look of your new kitchen, but trust me, you will think it was completely worth your time in the end. It will help everyone be on the same page. Your cabinetmaker will know what you want and there will be no confusion about your expectations. Plus YOU are committed to stand by your choices.

WARNING! If you are not comfortable with your choices after going through this process, you are not ready to start building. Take more time, let it settle awhile, then revisit it a month later. Remodeling is hard, emotionally and financially. You need to be ready to pull the trigger and be committed to seeing the project through.

 ## Dealing with Constraints

At about this point, you might really want to pull out your hair. Maybe you tried to do the storyboard but it just keeps getting more and more stuff on it! You just can't decide between a cabinet color or style, you've got three flooring choices, and so many paint swatches they won't all fit! But don't worry, you've just run head-on into my next section. When I see clients getting stuck in this area, I know it's time to show them that constraints can actually help, moving them further down the road towards their dream kitchen.

Because we live in America and are surrounded by abundance, having unlimited choices should make it easier right? But actually it doesn't. Research has shown that having too many choices is demotivating! It's true. Having too many options actually makes it harder to pick something you will feel good about. Using simple constraints will help you to filter what will actually work for you and enable you to focus on what you really need and want.

Useful constraints to apply:

- Timing

- Size

- Budget

- Water / electrical / gas hookups

- Color

- Style

- Appliances

- Physical limits

- Particular features

Constraints can be your friends!

Eva & Elaine

Let's check on Eva and Elaine to see how constraints might help them complete their storyboards.

Eva:

Size: Her kitchen is a fairly small L-shape with limited wall space. Her wall oven currently takes up a large space. She can't afford to move walls or change the location of the stove or the sink.

Color: Her living room has light colors. Because she can see the kitchen from the living room, she doesn't want a big color contrast in the kitchen.

Style: She really loves old furniture and also wants a light airy feel.

Appliances: She has white appliances and they are fairly new, so she'd like to keep them.

Eva & Elaine (cont.)

Timing: She has time and flexibility.

Budget: It was really hard to save $23,500, and her daughter is going to college in a month so she will not have access to more funds. She really has to make it work within this budget.

As you can see by **Eva**'s list, her overall budget is $23,500. She wants to go with a light or white cabinet color because it is visible from the adjoining room. So even though she has a beautiful chestnut cabinet color on her storyboard, she will remove that and instead focus on what extra feature she could add to white cabinets to give them more of a furniture feel. Later she may be able to add in a little chestnut accent color after the big decisions have been made. She has time to look around and since she is not getting new appliances, she would really like to find a

Elaine:

Size: She has a large U-shaped kitchen and likes the overall size. She just feels that it should be easier to use because she can never find anything.

Color: Both she and her husband want different colors. She likes light and he wants dark cabinets. Maybe they can compromise and do a darker island?

Style: They both like traditional and want it to complement the rest of their home.

Appliances: They want to buy a Wolf stove but have heard it can be expensive. This may take a large portion of the budget, so they might need to compromise on something else. It also might affect the rest of their choices so they need to get a real number for this stove first.

Timing: They have an anniversary party planned at their house in *three months*. This is a really tight schedule and they may need to make concessions to get this done.

Budget: They have $56,000 put away but may need access to more money in order to get all of the work done in the time they have.

way to add in a pantry. She can now confidently concentrate on an exact type of white cabinet, something with a furniture feel that keeps the space airy.

Elaine on the other hand has now recognizes timing is the number one factor. She has more room in her budget, but she also has some expensive appliances listed. Since she is unsure of the cost at this point, she will leave the Wolf stove on her board and keep researching. After thinking about it, both she and her husband agreed that cabinet color isn't really that critical. They've settled on a beautiful birch that is a light color for her but has the wood features that he likes. Because they realize timing is the big issue now, they can move off of cabinet color and start fine-tuning the other items. They pick a lovely countertop color with a little bit of contrast and are now ready to start figuring out the actual layout they want.

Layout with DFIO

After designing your preliminary storyboard, you have an idea of colors and finishes. You've looked into specific details about the items. At this point, you probably have a good idea of what you want the "outside" to look like. You should know the basic color and style of the cabinets, countertops, and floor. You might still be deciding on appliance models, but you know where they are going to be in the layout. So now we are ready to go back to the features list and try to incorporate as many of those as we can in the actual layout of the cabinetry.

This is a two-step process. First, I want you to draw a very simple sketch as though you are looking at your kitchen from above. We need back wall measurements, appliance locations and size, and where your sink and stove are each located. These are the basic components that will determine what is available for new cabinetry.

Step One:

- Draw a simple picture of your kitchen from above. Start with the outside length of the walls where cabinets and appliances are located. Don't worry about being precise. Just get an approximate idea of what you have to work with.

- Add fixed items that can't be moved. For example, the sink, stove, refrigerator and dishwasher. These will be standard sizes. Sink (36″), stove (30″ or 36″), refrigerator (36″) and dishwasher (24″).

- All base cabinets will be twenty-four inches deep and uppers will be twelve inches deep. Mark those dimensions on your drawing.

- Mark door openings, and any other areas where you aren't be able to have cabinets.

Now that we know the basic layout of existing cabinets, you can modify this sketch based on the new features you want to add. *My first priority is to figure out the base cabinets and to get as many drawer units as I can, leaving room for a pantry space, garbage pullout, and cookie sheet door, if needed.* I also account for sink and stove cabinets.

Step Two:

Here is a brief checklist for inserting the Nine Features of a Great Kitchen:

- Draw soft-closing doors with "handles like jewelry" (Features 1 and 8) and note which way you want the doors to open to ensure there are no crowded or blocked areas.

- Add pot/pan drawer base units (Feature 2) symmetrically, usually to the left and right of the stove or refrigerator location. Try to fit drawers that are at least twenty-four inches wide. Typically I try to fit in a pair of thirty inch or thirty-six inch base drawers.

- Locate your spice insert (Feature 3), probably in one of the top drawers of a base cabinet next to the stove.

- Add pantry unit (Feature 5) if possible, twenty-four inches wide. Remember that the pantry unit takes up floor-to-ceiling space.

- Your Tupperware (Feature 6) will go under pantry unit.

- Add cookie sheet cabinet (Feature 7), usually a twelve inch cabinet.

- If possible add refrigerator cabinet (Feature 9). Budget forty inches for the cabinet to fit a thirty-six inch refrigerator).

- Fill in with upper cabinets to match the base cabinets.

- Add garbage pullout (Feature 4). Remember you need twenty-three inches to fit a double-can cabinet.

For a free ebook about how to organize your items in the new space, visit *www.divinekitchen.net/good-organization*.

Now you should have a physical representation of what you like both inside and out. The **"inside"** portion is the layout we just discussed showing how the new cabinets will function and incorporating as many of my Nine Features as possible. Your storyboard shows the **"outside"** colors, finishes, and any other details needed to determine the cost. You can now move confidently into the next section, knowing that the design you have developed will hold all the essential items in your kitchen, with much greater access and visibility. And at the same time, you are confident the "pretty" part matches what you like and you no longer have to keep looking at hundreds of options.

As you will see in the next few pages, Eva and Elaine have worked hard to integrate the nine features into their existing floor plan. They are not moving any appliances or adding any space by moving walls. Instead they are able to transform their kitchen by adding the most important element, soft closing drawers. After finding space for those, they moved onto adding all the other elements, thus changing the synergy of their existing space.

Now that they have completed that section they are ready to determine how much their designs will cost and learn about all the materials that go into their kitchen.

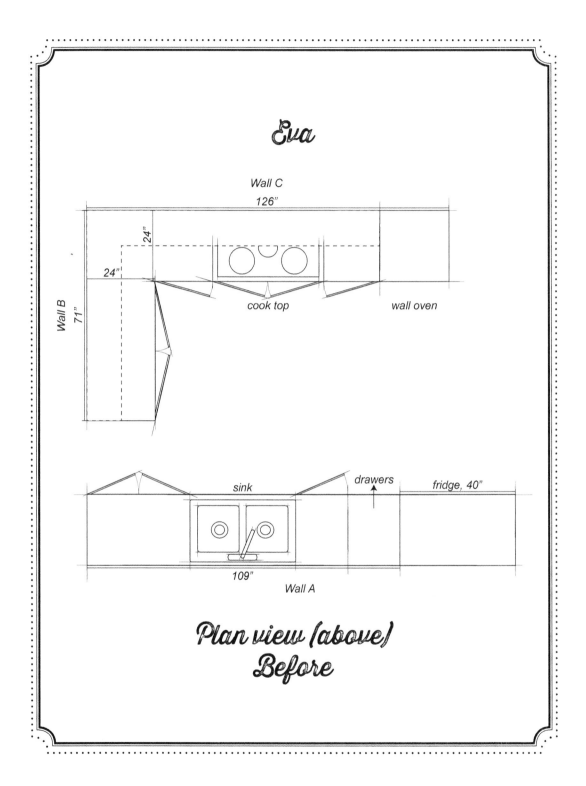

Eva

Wall C

126"

24"

24"

Wall B
71"

cook top

wall oven

drawers

fridge, 40"

sink

109"

Wall A

Plan view (above)
Before

Eva (cont.)

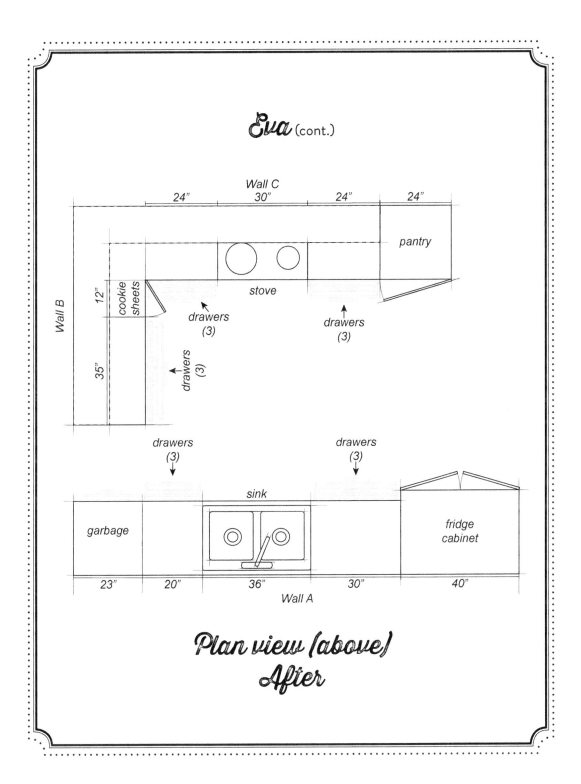

Wall C

24"   30"   24"   24"

pantry

Wall B

12"   cookie sheets

stove

drawers (3)

drawers (3)

35"   drawers (3)

drawers (3)   drawers (3)

sink

garbage

fridge cabinet

23"   20"   36"   30"   40"

Wall A

Plan view (above)
After

Eva (cont.)

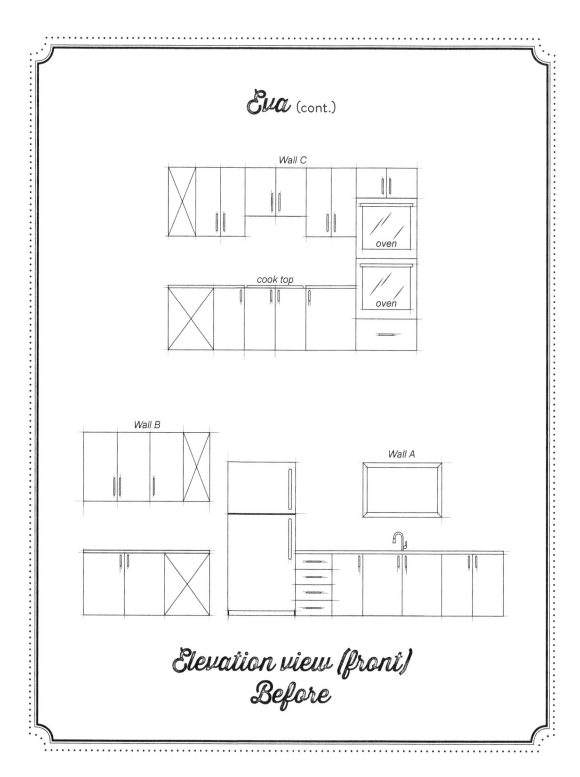

Wall C

oven

oven

cook top

Wall B

Wall A

Elevation view (front) Before

Eva (cont.)

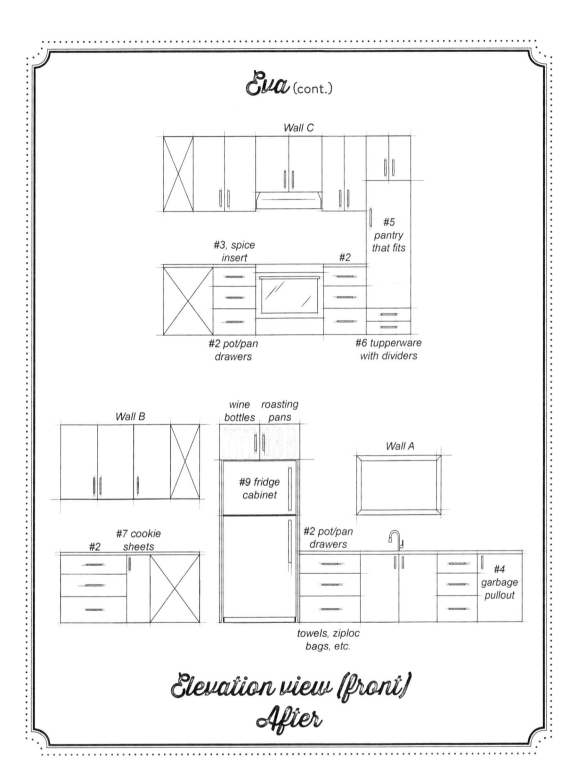

Wall C

#3, spice insert

#2

#5 pantry that fits

#2 pot/pan drawers

#6 tupperware with dividers

Wall B

wine bottles   roasting pans

#9 fridge cabinet

Wall A

#7 cookie sheets

#2

#2 pot/pan drawers

#4 garbage pullout

towels, ziploc bags, etc.

Elevation view (front) After

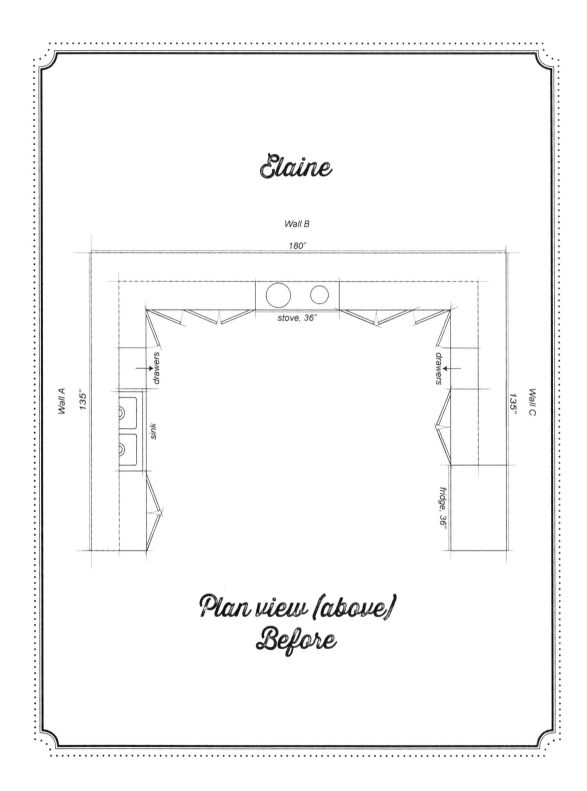

Elaine

Wall B

180"

stove, 36"

Wall A

135"

drawers

sink

drawers

Wall C

135"

fridge, 36"

Plan view (above)
Before

Elaine (cont.)

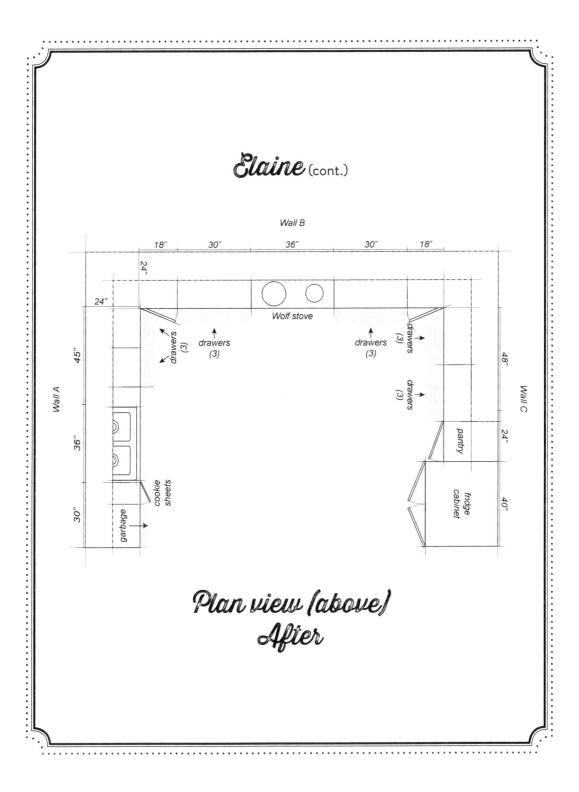

Wall B

18" 30" 36" 30" 18"

24"

24"

Wolf stove

Wall A

45"

36"

30"

drawers (3)

drawers (3)

drawers (3)

drawers (3)

drawers (3)

cookie sheets

garbage

Wall C

48"

24"

40"

pantry

fridge cabinet

Plan view (above)
After

Elaine (cont.)

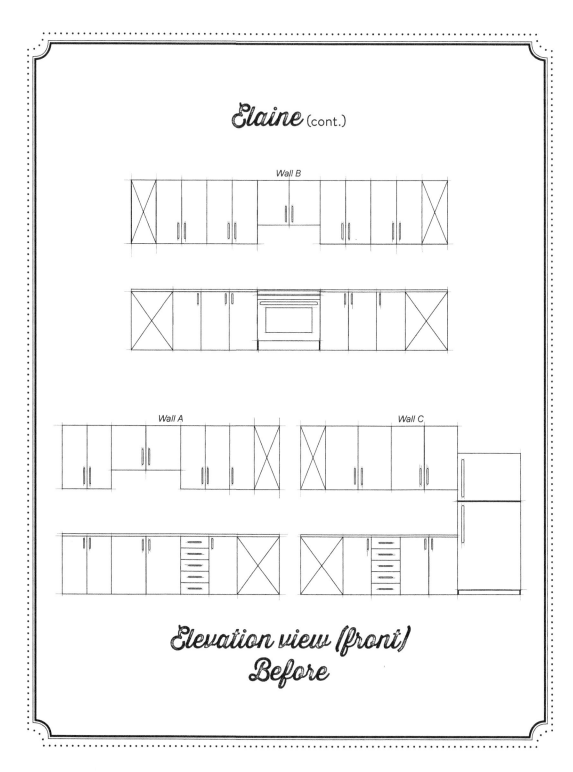

Elevation view (front)
Before

Elaine (cont.)

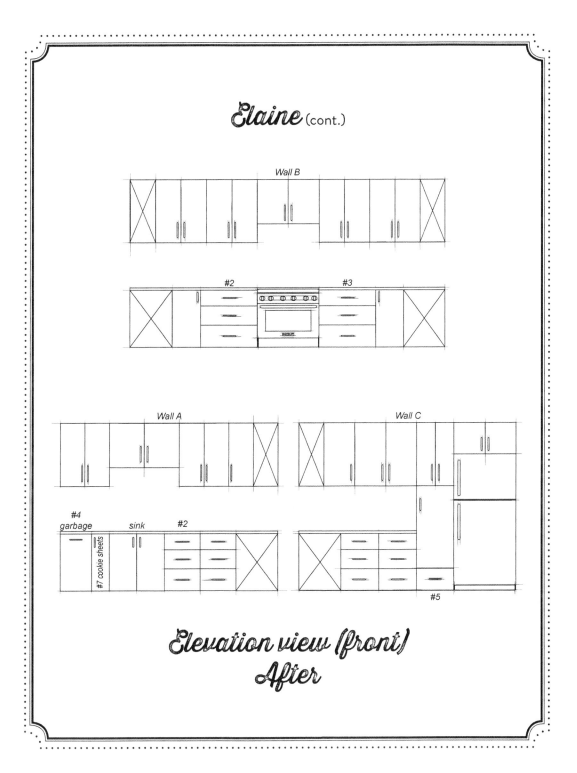

Wall B

#2   #3

Wall A   Wall C

#4
garbage   sink   #2

#7 cookie sheets

#5

Elevation view (front)
After

Determining Your Budget
So, How Much Will My Beautiful Design Cost?"

Now that you have a good idea of what you want your kitchen to look like from the inside out, you probably want to know what it will actually cost. Let's talk about how to price out a kitchen. This can feel a little overwhelming so I find it's best to concentrate your time and budget on the bigger items first, nail those down and then worry about the smaller stuff afterwards. If you treat everything with the same importance, you will drive yourself nuts trying to balance it all.

So what constitutes a big item? Well, for me it comes down to three main things: cabinetry, countertops, and appliances. This is for a couple of reasons. First they generally cost the most, second they take the longest to build and so have the longest lead time, and finally they are the things you touch and use every day.

In addition, many contractors believe you are on a "need-to-know basis"—meaning what you don't know will cost *you*. So it's important to be as well-informed on the big items as possible.

 ## Basic Items in a Kitchen Remodel

Below is a (simplified) chart which shows the nine components that go into a typical full kitchen remodel. These are the most important details that make up the budget. They are in order of most expensive to least.

Working Budget

ITEM	POSSIBLE "HIDDEN" COSTS	AVERAGE COST	TIMELINE (3 MONTHS)
Cabinetry		$10,000	$$$$$
Countertops		$5–6,000	$$$
Appliances		$4–10,000	$$$$
Flooring		$6,000	$$
Electrical	*	$2,000	$
Plumbing	*	$1,000	$
Sheetrock	*	$1,500	$
Tile		$1,500	$
Paint		$1,000	$

You will want to have a basic understanding of each of these and their actual costs so that you can accurately pick what will fit within your budget.

It is important that you are educated on the items shown on the above chart. That's why I am providing a brief explanation of the critical things in each section along with a range of costs. This is in no way exhaustive but is meant to give you some perspective based on my years of experience. After each section, you can refer to the more detailed explanations at the back of this book in the index.

Before we discuss kitchen remodeling costs in depth, notice the three items on the chart marked with an asterisk (*) under hidden costs. I find on every job these items catch customers by surprise. Either it is assumed they are included in the bid or they don't realize the amount of work involved in each. Be warned that a good kitchen remodel includes each of these and you will need to include them in your budget or you will be surprised—and not in a good way. Plumbing and electrical work must fix any existing problems and bring your kitchen up to current code and safety regulation. New sheetrock and texture is usually required to repair damage and make the kitchen look new.

Education Is Free

There are dozens of components that go into a kitchen remodel. It can feel overwhelming to sort through it all and make all of those decisions. This next section will teach you about the various components of your remodel so you can understand what is on your storyboard and eventually the associated cost of each item. Let's start with what I think are the three bare minimum pieces of information you need to research. Just remember, it's free to educate yourself, so take the time to understand what you are buying. It will be the most cost-effective time you will spend in this process.

So let's talk about these three "big" items first and then move on to the rest. What I will ask you to do is after learning about each item, is refer back to your storyboard, and identify which type of product you originally picked out. Then, using what you learned, start estimating the cost of each and transfer it to your *working budget*.

Remember that this is a process, so as you learn about each product and get some numbers, don't worry if they seem too high. This is just so you understand what some things cost in relation to others. Once you know what you are looking for, you can always get multiple bids to see if you can find a lower price.

The reason this is so important is so that you can competently compare bids. If you do not understand what makes up each bid, you definitely cannot compare them to pick the best product AND make sure you are getting what you are paying for. I find most women get ripped off because of this one thing!

"Big" Item No. 1: Cabinetry

Cabinetry is usually the most complex and expensive item in your kitchen. The bottom line is that your kitchen cabinets are being priced using six different components whether you understand them or not. Every cabinetmaker uses these six components to determine the price of each job. Traditionally, the industry used a Linear Foot pricing model, so it was easier to compare bids. But these days not everyone uses that model, and there are many ways that cabinetmakers bid jobs. For instance, my shop does not bid by linear foot. Instead we have our own model, starting with how much the products cost, plus labor, plus profit per job. But no matter how a cabinetmaker is bidding the job, the following is part of how he or she calculates the final number.

In order to understand how the cabinetmaker got to the price they are giving you, being familiar with these six components will give you a large part of the equation. When you start comparing bids, you will be able to accurately pick the best person for your job. All kitchen cabinets are comprised of the following components: cabinet box (carcass), frame, door/drawer front, drawer boxes, hardware, and finish.

Because there is so much variety in quality and price within each of these six components, the price can vary widely. By understanding what makes up each part, you will better understand the overall finished price of each bid. More importantly, this is also one of those areas where a lot of consumers get ripped off. Some dishonest contractors swap premium woods for less expensive woods, change components and hardware for cheaper versions, and the consumer is none the wiser.

Some common cabinetmaker tricks might be things like selling one type of cabinet box and then switching it to a lower-grade box. You might be sold a certain wood species for the door and get a lower-level quality of wood when your doors are made. You might be told that you're getting premium cabinets with a high bid, but in reality they are what I would call budget materials.

When you know just a few things about the materials, you will be able to see what grade of cabinet that you were actually sold.

In the chart below, you can see what is considered the two basic levels of cabinets. This is a simplification, but in general these features apply. And depending on the quality of wood being used or detailing, some of the items can fall into both categories. For further details about all the components that make up a set of kitchen cabinets, **check the reference library**.

COMPONENTS		BUDGET	PREMIUM
Box		½" ply	¾" ply
Face frame		X	X
	inset		X
	overlay	X	X
Frameless		¾" laminate	¾" laminate
Door/drawer fronts		lower-grade wood	premium hardwoods
Drawer box		plywood or press board (laminate)	solid wood dovetail
Hardware		ball bearing, Chinese import	soft-closing, Blum, European style hinges
	handles	4"	6"–9"
Finish		Low-grade lacquer, paint	conversion varnish, sprayed
	glazed doors		X

"Big" Item No. 2: Countertops

The second most important component is countertops—which one to choose and how much your selection will cost. Though it's not always the most expensive out of the total budget, often it is. For most families, new cabinets and countertops take up the majority of their budget. This makes counter-tops very important, and there are many things to learn in order to make an informed decision. I feel the industry does a horrible job of actually explaining the basics of countertops and how they are priced. So this section will start the discussion and hopefully provide some basic perspective.

There are three basic types of countertops used in most households today. Despite the industry telling you that there are a thousand options, those options are typically used for fancier kitchens and for people who are trying to do something different. Most families select engineered stone, granite, or, if they need to save some money, a Corian-type, solid-surface product. Remember, the industry makes its money by constantly coming up with more color options and details but that doesn't mean you have to buy any of it.

So let me explain what I feel the industry does a poor job of communicating—the difference between the three products. Engineered stone is made from crushed quartz and is *man-made*. Granite is cut out of the Earth and as such, is *natural* with quality and color varying tremendously. Corian-like products are made of very hard *plastic*s. Corian products can vary widely in color and price, and significant strides have been made towards copying the look of the previous two.

The reason it can be really confusing when shopping at the stores and looking at samples is that all the manufacturers *copy each other's style* and colors. This makes it extremely difficult for the average person to tell what is what. Use the following descriptions below to educate yourself so you know what you are touching.

Engineered stone

It is man-made, with consistent quality and colors. Non-porous and the hardest surface, you can cut on it, put hot pots on it, and it needs no sealing. Price for an average job, including a four inch backsplash, is around $5,000–$6,000.

Bottom line: Great choice for all applications if you can afford it. Style-wise it is typically known for having a *consistent quartz appearance*.

Granite

Color and quality vary tremendously because granite is a natural stone milled from all around the globe. Prices range widely based on supply and demand, so popular or hard-to-get colors will cost more. Granite is very hard. You can cut on it and put hot pots on it. It needs minimal sealing depending on color and type. *But* it is not a huge deal like the industry makes it out to be. Price for an average job is $5,000–$6,000, which includes a four inch backsplash.

Bottom line: Great choice for all applications. Style-wise it has a wide variety of "natural" features, so a lot of time and attention should be paid to visiting the slab yard with door samples before selecting the final slab. *Do not leave this choice up to your fabricator.*

Corian-like solid surfaces

Very hard polyesters make up this product that has many uses both residentially and commercially. It is a wonderful product to create a truly seamless look because field seams (places where countertops are connected) are invisible and sinks can be fully integrated (without seams). The upside is that it can be a beautiful look and save you money. The downside is that you cannot cut directly on its surface and you can't place hot pots on it. Most women use a small potholder or trivet and a cutting board to solve these problems. Prices range between $3,500–4,000.

Bottom line: This is the most affordable product and it has a seamless consistent look. The best choice if your budget is limited.

To get more details about how countertops are made, pricing, and what specifically makes up a bid for each type, check the reference library.

"Big" Item No. 3: Appliances

One of the more frustrating things about kitchen remodeling is pricing appliances. In the last twenty years, it seems they just keep getting more and more complicated. So many options and variations make it hard to keep track of what is really important. Use my chart below to get a basic idea of cost of the items on your storyboard and then research each for specific pricing in your area.

This can be a bit overwhelming, so to whittle this down to a manageable size, here is some information based on what I see average families buy. I have also provided some size guidelines so that you are prepared to go out and research more fully. More detailed explanations and suggestions about appliances can be found in the reference library.

APPLIANCE			STANDARD SIZE (WIDTH)	PRICE
Refrigerator			36″	
	French door			$2,000–$4,000
	countertop depth			$2,000–$9,000
Stove				
	freestanding	Gas	30″, 36″, 48″	$2,500–$8,000
		Electric	30″, 36″	$2,500–$4,000
	slide-in	gas/electric	30″, 36″, 48″	$3,000–$6,000
	hood/micro unit		30″	$500
	hood (typical)		30″	$200
	hood (specialty)		30″, 36″, 48″	$800–$8,000
Wall Oven	double		30″	$4,000–$8,000
Dishwasher	standard		24″	$250
	with matching cabinet panel			$700

Now that we've discussed the "big three" we can discuss the six additional components that are most commonly part of a kitchen remodel.

Flooring

You will find a wide range of flooring options. Be aware that the best solution may depend upon the climate where you live. Because I live in California in a dry area, it is more accepted to install wood floors in kitchen areas. But that might not work for your location or it might be cost-prohibitive to have it installed correctly. So I will talk about a range of flooring and how it is priced but please do your own research on your local conditions to discover what the best options are for you. For further details see the reference library.

There are three basic options for your kitchen floor: hardwood, engineered wood, and tile.

I would not suggest using solid hardwood in a kitchen area, but there are people who do. I much prefer engineered wood. Engineered wood has a plywood substrate and real hardwood on top. It is much more stable around small amounts of moisture and it is very durable. Engineered wood is also much less expensive to install (materials and labor) without sacrificing the beauty of hardwood. I prefer a glue-down application most of the time. It reduces the echo sound and feels great under your bare feet. On average we charge $4.50 per square foot for installation. You should budget $5.50 per square foot for materials.

To calculate a basic budget measure your kitchen's length and width. Multiply to get a square foot calculation. So if your kitchen measures fifteen feet by fifteen feet, the room's square footage is two hundred and twenty-five square feet (15′ × 15′ = 225′ sq. ft.).

Hardwood Quote

225′ × $4.50/sq. ft. installation = $1,012.50

225′ × $5.50/sq. ft. materials = $1,237.50

Total Estimated = $2,250

Tile is another good option and probably more the norm. Customers usually assume that tile is less expensive, however my experience has been that often the labor price on tile installation is *more* expensive. So depending on where you live, the tile you choose, and the complexity of your job will ultimately determine the price for tile installation.

Prices range dramatically depending on where you live and the complexity of your job. So I will just use our area for the same size tile job so you can see a comparison.

Tile Quote:

225′ × $3.50/sq. ft., materials = $787.50

225′ × $6.00/sq. ft., labor = $1,350

Total estimate = $2,137.50

Electrical

When considering a kitchen remodel there are often "hidden" costs. As professionals they are not hidden to us since we know they will happen on every job. But for the average homeowner, who doesn't realize these behind-the-scenes components will also occur in the remodel, they may come as a surprise. Remember what makes your kitchen work behind the scenes is a combination of WATER and ELECTRICITY and the plumbing and electrical costs can add up. It makes sense to pay attention to these two very important areas.

The most common electrical expenses for kitchen remodeling include the following items. We typically add these to the kitchens we build. We always use a licensed electrician for this work, encountering and fixing many old problems.

TYPE OF ELECTRICAL		
Recessed lights		$1,500–$2,500
Updating/fixing outlets		$300
Add dedicated circuits	fridge, DW, stove	$500
Adding USB outlets		$100 each
Adding undercabinet LED lights		$500

Plumbing

Another "hidden" cost for the consumer is plumbing. In ninety percent of our jobs, we add the following plumbing tasks. Please be sure to use a licensed plumbing contractor with experience specifically in kitchen plumbing. I have seen so many jobs end poorly due to an inexperienced plumber.

Disconnect/hook up new sink		$350 plus parts
Hook up new dishwasher		$250 plus parts
Hook up water line to refrigerator		$150 plus parts
Install new gas line for stove Cooktops are ¾" Stoves are 1 ¼"	depends on distance to gas main	$500–$2,000

Further details can be found in the reference library.

We are almost done! We just have three more small sections to consider. Even though they make up a smaller portion of your budget, they are important in the overall finished look of your new kitchen. So please don't skip this part. Let's talk a bit about sheetrock/texture repair, backsplashes, and painting.

Sheetrock/Texture

In almost every kitchen remodeling project there is going to be sheetrock damage. This happens for a variety of reasons. For example, you will need sheetrock repair when you install new lighting, whether it is can lights or new fixtures. You will also often need repair when you remove old countertops, replace cabinets or need new outlets installed. Of course, that doesn't take into account moving walls, etc. This is one area where I see customers try to cut corners and it always ends poorly. If you are going to invest in your kitchen and buy beautiful cabinets and countertops and go through all that hassle, please do not skip this step!

Nothing ruins an otherwise beautiful job like a horrible sheetrock patch, either by the homeowner or a "cheap" contractor. On average, we spend about $1,500 per kitchen to get high-quality repair and retexture. It makes the room look brand new and you can't tell there was damage to the original sheetrock. A good texture job should be completely invisible.

If you're STILL not sure it's worth the money, imagine this.

You went to Nordstrom and bought a gorgeous new dress for your best friends' wedding. It took quite a few hours and between the matching shoes and earrings, you spent a chunk of change. The day of the wedding arrives and as you are getting dressed you realize you forgot to buy nylons. What do you do?

You look around and find an old pair, but after putting them on there are huge holes in them and tears up both sides. Would you ever walk into a very fancy wedding all decked out—except for the huge holes in your nylons? They would stand out like a sore thumb and probably every person you talked to would ask if you were in an accident on the way to the wedding.

Of course that would never happen. You would take the last extra step and buy a good quality pair. That way, people would notice your gorgeous dress and shoes, not what your legs look like. This is what sheetrock repair is like. It is a step you will not notice if it is done well, but one that will stare you in the face every time you go into your kitchen if it's done poorly. Check the reference library for more information.

Sheetrock/texture: $1,500–$2,000 depending on original condition and damage.

Tile Backsplash

This is an option that can add a lot of punch to a simple kitchen. Price varies depending on the type of tile you select and the complexity of your design. Some things that add to the price are how many outlets the tile setter has to cut around, any special moldings, or any customization. On average, our clients pay $1,500–$2,000 for materials and labor for a typical backsplash going behind two or three walls.

Painting

This final section is another one that I've found to be difficult for customers. In the beginning, all they can think about is paint color, so they rush out to start picking out colors, but this is the typically the least expensive part of the job and the easiest to change. So I suggest that they get paint swatches to help with defining their overall style and look on their storyboard, but not pick any actual accent colors until very close to the end of the remodel.

This is for a couple of reasons. The first is that most of the room should be painted a neutral color, and you won't have a clear idea of the accent colors until some of the new items are installed, specifically the cabinets and countertops. It gets expensive to have to repaint if you are hiring a professional. It is much better to allow the new space to take shape and then you will be confident in your selection.

The second reason is that paint is just the backdrop. It is not supposed to stand out. A common mistake is to have $100 worth of paint, overtake $25,000 worth of cabinets and countertops. A good rule of thumb is what costs the most should stand out the most. Your judicious use of an accent color should complement where you spend the bulk of your money, not compete with it.

Finally, I suggest that you paint your ceiling a soft white (Swiss Coffee) in a flat finish. It will hide any small defects and will make your room look much taller.

Painting: $1,500–$2,000, depending on size of space if a professional painter is involved.

So remember at the beginning of this chapter when we started on a working budget? Now it's time for you to start putting your own proposed numbers into the budget. Just write down what you know and estimate what you don't. This will start the process and get you thinking about which items are most important to include for your family.

Working Budget

	MATERIALS	LABOR	DETAILS	PROPOSED	ACTUAL
Cabinetry					
Countertops					
Appliances					
Flooring					
Electrical					
Plumbing					
Sheetrock / texture					
Backsplash tile					
Paint					
TOTALS					

To download a PDF of this chart, visit *www.divinekitchen.net/budget.*

How To Get Bids
Fine-Tuning Your Budget

Now that you've learned about all the materials and have a storyboard of what you like, you will need to have a process for hiring qualified contractors. Whether you want to manage the process yourself or hire a general contractor, you will still need to understand the bidding process. Remember the story at the beginning about planning a huge important party? You didn't feel comfortable just asking a friend or neighbor to make a few appetizers, right? Now is the time to make sure that the bids you get are accurate, comparable, and fair. This will ensure that you hire the right person for the job at the right price.

One of the first decisions you must make before moving forward is whether you are going to do the management of the remodel yourself or hire a professional to manage it for you.

What Is a General Contractor?

This is confusing for most people and I don't blame them. In my fathers' day, a general contractor handled all portions of a job. He figured out the design of the project with the customer, hired the subcontractors and specialty trades, was on the job site every day, checked for quality and basically managed every part of the job until it was "delivered" to the customer. This meant he paid the workers, he fired the workers if they weren't capable, and took on all the responsibility of the job. Nowadays the term has gotten really muddied and can mean a lot of different things. In kitchen remodeling, it can be even more confusing. What follows is my opinion. You will need to speak clearly with the people who are going through the interview and hiring process to make sure your expectations are clear and if they can meet them.

To me, a general contractor who specializes in kitchens does the following:

- Hires, manages, and pays all subcontractors including cabinetmaker, countertops fabricator/installer, appliance installation, flooring specialists, electricians, and plumbers.

- Typically brings you samples or introduces you to subcontractors to help with design, and figuring out layout and overall look.

- Orders materials and appliances.

- Schedules the tradespeople.

- Inspects subcontractors for quality control.

I have worked on many jobs where the general contractor also does the rough work, plumbing, and electrical, basically getting the job site ready for the cabinetmaker and countertop fabricator. In this case, the cabinetmaker would work and get paid directly from the homeowner but coordinate with the general contractor.

It is important to know that **typically** the general contractor gets paid a ten to twenty percent markup of anybody that he or she brings onto the job site. Customers squirm when they hear that because they think it's a lot of money for nothing. But remember *the general contractor* is taking on all the responsibility of the job site. For that fee, she or he is supposed to manage the day-to-day operations, quality control, and all the behind-the-scenes problems; make sure that all the subcontractors get paid; and the job makes consistent progress. It is a lot of work to do and it's a big responsibility. So if he or she is good at that job, it is well worth the money.

So, DIY or Hire a General Contractor?

If you decide to perform the general contractor role yourself, it will require that you do all of the hiring and firing that the general contractor does. It requires that you be available, patient, and a good manager.

Later in this book when we talk about making your dream kitchen a reality, I describe how to be a successful general contractor. Whether you will be the general contractor or you will hire one, you will need to know how to get bids.

Getting Bids

Getting good bids can be a frustrating experience but it's a necessary one. Very few people are honest about this important part of doing a remodel. So, I will give you my opinion of what I think is important. I am not going to sugarcoat it, this is the unvarnished version!

The most common complaints I hear from customers are 1) it takes too long to get a bid back from the contractor and 2) they never received a call back with a bid. This is traditionally the way contractors behave and I believe that it has to change. But those frustrations are only some of the problems I see daily as an industry professional. What I also see are vague, general bids that just contain totals, but no real detail. The pool of experienced contractors is also small, making your choices limited. All of these reasons combined are why so many homeowners end up being dissatisfied with their contractor.

You can create a better experience for yourself. But you have to follow certain steps and take responsibility for your remodel. Here are my guidelines for getting a complete, accurate bid in a timely manner.

Step One: *Set a realistic amount of time for getting bids.* Do not think you are just going to call a few people and get bids within a two-week period. It's not going to happen. Instead, accept that the speed and accuracy of your bids are dependent on you and how prepared you are. When you have a thorough understanding of what you want and clear expectations, your will receive a more accurate bid more quickly.

Step Two: *Draw from a large source of mixed information.* Type up a big list from the phone book, call your friends, and look at various online resources like Angie's List and houzz.com. Understand that, out of all those on your list, many won't even return your call, a few will miss their appointments, and a few will show up but never submit a bid. If you just start with three guys and then are left choosing between the late guy and the one you don't like, well, that's not a very good way to start a large project.

Step Three: *Type up a short but complete script detailing the needs of your project.* It should include your budget range, when you expect to start the project, and when you will be making your contractor selection. Leaving an open-ended conversation with no time limit on the contractor is a sure way to get no results. Showing that you have thought out your needs will make it faster and easier for a contractor to develop a bid. If you are still in the development stage and trying to determine the look and shape, show as much of what you want up front as you can so they will believe you are serious. As contractors, we are being called every day to visit new jobs. There is never a convenient time for us, since we are always in the middle of someone else's job. You will get a better response if we don't feel like our time has been wasted.

Step Four: *Call all of the people on your list using a script and set up appointments.* Be sure to tell them you have a storyboard with what you want your kitchen to look like, and that you plan to make a decision by _____ date. Be sure to include what items you expect to be on the bid to ensure you are comparing apples to apples. Tell the contractor you want the bid broken down by materials and labor or any other details to make it easy for you to compare bids.

This is when the hiring process starts! Right here. On your list, keep track of who answered their phone. Who called you back? Who showed up on time? How they do anything is how they'll do everything, so even a seemingly minor "infraction" like being late will demonstrate how they will be on your job. The responsive nature (or lack thereof) of each contractor sets the tempo for the job.

If you are all over the place and disorganized, they will sense this and many will take advantage of your ignorance. Some of the best professionals may not want to work with you, because they already have a schedule full of good clients. *If you are organized and clear about what you want, you will get much, much more accurate bids, and you'll get a faster response from the best contractors.*

You should also be aware that getting bids from cabinetmakers is different from getting a bid from an electrician. The amount of money you will be spending on each design element and with each subcontractor varies widely. Plan for things to take longer for larger-dollar bids and be faster for smaller ones because they don't take as much time to figure out.

A word of caution, it is considered very rude to schedule back-to-back appointments from competing contractors. You will shoot yourself in the foot if you do this. You should always respect that each contractor deserves a block of time to speak with you privately without another competitor waiting in the wings. If you attempt to do this, thinking it will lower your price, it will backfire. You will only get bids from contractors who do not care about you or your job, have little respect for you, and only care about the money. If you want someone who respects you and your needs, show that same level of respect to them.

In addition, beware of contractors promising really quick turnarounds. This means low quality nearly every time and that their emphasis is not where it should be—on quality. The last thing you want is to spend lots of money, have loads of emotional upheaval, and, then when it's all over, find low-quality, sloppy, shoddy work all over the place.

Step Five: *Qualify your desired contractor.* Now comes the fun part. You've had your appointments and talked with a lot of contractors. You've set a date for determining your selection to ensure that those who are really interested will develop and submit a bid in a timely fashion. Now it's time to qualify those bids. Here's what to do with all those bids you received.

Sorting and Weighing Bids

The biggest problem I see with customers when they are choosing a contractor is that they compare bids that are not complete or similar. Basically they are only comparing totals. I see it all the time and it just doesn't work very well.

This stems from two things. First, customers are vague and uneducated about what they want and second, there are a lot of unscrupulous contractors out there who take advantage of a customers' ignorance. Do not be one of these women!

So if you specified clearly what you wanted and you told each contractor you wanted their bid broken down by materials and labor, this section will be much easier for you. Here is the way I compare bids.

I split the piles of bids into three groups by price. I read through each bid noticing the details and comparing the prices of each. I sort them by lowest, middle, and highest price.

Next, I refer back to my notes about each contractor and make a note about how I liked his or her personality, responsiveness, and character. Out of that group, I usually pick the two people I liked the most, and who seemed the most interested in my project and me. I compare those quotes to each other.

If my number-one choice is the highest in price I will usually call that person back for a second meeting. At that meeting I will explain my concerns and ask for an explanation as to why this bid is "$****" much more than everyone else's. If he or she will negotiate, seems interested, and we can come to an understanding, then that is who I will likely choose. If he or she is unresponsive or rude, I will probably hire the second one in my lineup if their references check out. Remember, at this second meeting, I am not just trying to get a lower price. I am trying to discover the reason for the difference. If there is a legitimate reason and a reasonable explanation, then I will choose the higher-priced contractor.

After I have two or three reasonable quotes price-wise, I continue my qualifying procedure by looking at their job photos and calling their references list.

How To Check References

Most women are uncomfortable calling strangers and asking personal questions. So here are my suggestions to make this process easier. Accept that you must call a minimum of three references. **Do not skip this step!** Most customers ask for references and then get caught up in the excitement of the job or let their anxiety minimize the importance. When you call these three references, I would start with more general casual questions and then go into more in-depth questions as you build up a rapport. Don't be afraid to dig a little deeper.

You should go through this selection process for all the work that entails materials and labor or for any amount over $1,500. Obviously, I would spend much more time on my cabinet contractor selection and less on my sheetrock guy based on the amount in my budget.

In the next section (Section 8: Implementing Your Plan), I go into more detail about the hiring process. I talk about contracts, the selection process, and how to protect yourself. Those are very important too, but for now, we'll keep the discussion to bids and the selection process.

To illustrate good and bad bids and why you need to pay careful attention to them, let's take a look at the bids Eva received. For the sake of this book, the bid is simplified and doesn't include items like tax, and specific details about the company.

One of the bids below is thorough and complete, and the other is what I would call a poor bid. It basically just has a total. A bid with just a total doesn't necessarily mean that the *quality* will be poor, but if you are spending $15,000 on cabinets, wouldn't you want to know the details? How high is the quality of the material? What hardware will they use? Do you feel comfortable with this company? It is often very hard to discern that from a poorly done bid.

Sample script for interviewing references:

Hi Mary,

I'm _____ and I was given your name as a reference by _____. I was wondering if I could ask you a few questions about the kitchen they did for you. Great, I'll just take a few minutes of your time. My first question is. . . .

Casual questions:

Did you like working with _____?

Were you happy with the job?

What did you like about working with _____?

Did _____ answer their phone and respond to questions well?

Do you feel _____ listened to you and understood your needs?

Deeper questions:

Do you feel you got what you paid for?

What would you have done differently?

Do you feel your vision and overall design was met?

Do you feel _____ managed the job effectively?

How did _____ handle problems and issues when they came up?

Overall, would you hire _____ again to work on another project?

Another thing that I feel should be on the bid is what won't be included in the scope of work. Conflict and problems arise when you make assumptions about what the contractor will be doing. For instance, it is well known in the industry that if you are acting as your own general contractor or you have hired one, the general contractor is responsible for all of the many transitional steps between individual vendors, not each specific trade. So getting upset at your cabinetmaker for a misstep that is your responsibility (or the general contractor's) is a waste of time and is sure to frustrate him or her.

Always ask about this because it is common for customers to assume we, as contractors, will take care of everything. In fact many of the underlying things we as consumers lump into "taking care of everything" are not a contractor's responsibility and are usually set by building codes and industry standards.

Be certain to ask what is NOT included in the bid. A good example is demolition of existing cabinets. It is typically not included. Companies that tell you it is are just charging you within the bid. When in doubt, ASK.

Good Bid

Johnson Cabinets *Location* *License #*	
Not included: Demo of existing cabinets and hook up of plumbing	
Style: Inset	
Materials: Inset white cabinets, 45LF with Shaker door, name "Bella." Added detail A. Beaded-F1. Customer request furniture feet, style roman 1. Std all cabinets. Adjustable shelves std. 3 ½" crown molding std. 36" uppers std, 34 ½" base cabinets. ¾" prefinished maple insides, unpainted bottoms, 2" light rail included. Dovetail birch drawer boxes std. Blum full-extension slides std. Blum hinges std.	$13,200
Finish: Conversion varnish-Swiss coffee white	
Installation	$2,000.00
Total Bid	$15,200
Performance Payments	30% deposit, 30% when installation starts, remainder due after final walk-through.
Estimated Delivery: *6–7 weeks from deposit*	

Bad Bid

Bob's Cabinets	
Materials:	
White Shaker cabinets	
with shelves	
Customer to pick color	
To be delivered	
All cabinets standard, drawers and slides.	
Total Bid	$14,000
Estimated Delivery:	

As you can see this would be very confusing. How can she possibly compare the total numbers if the details (materials and labor) are not the same? And yet, eighty-five percent of the time I see customers choose this second bid simply because it is lower.

Let's pretend that another new kitchen hopeful, Elizabeth, chose the lowest bid. One month later, the cabinets show up and they are not at all what she wanted. They are not inset, they don't have any of the details they "verbally" discussed. Bob, the cabinetmaker is mad at her because she is upset. He argues with her about previous conversations and is adamant that he delivered what they agreed upon. He installs the cabinets and demands payment.

After Bob leaves, Elizabeth starts to put her stuff away, still upset but not knowing what else to do. She notices that the shelves are fixed and she can't fit a lot of her items into the cabinets. The drawers don't close gently and they only come out part way. She looks more closely and sees that they are not Blum hinges and slides, as discussed. She starts to look more closely and sees there is just a small ugly molding on top of cabinets and all the doors slam shut. In trying to save money she didn't confirm that what she wanted was what was in the **written bid**. She only looked at the bottom line and ended up with cabinets that are as ineffective as what she had before, they are just white.

In our pretend scenario, the cabinets Bob installed are technically white and have Shaker doors but they are nothing like what Elizabeth wanted. The lesson here is to remember all of the materials, hardware, and details are what make the kitchen work. If those details are not in the bid, do not assume they will be included.

Eva

So let's check in with Eva and Elaine and see how far along they are in their working budget. Were they able to get good bids? Do they have a clear sense of how much their projects will cost? Let's see how they are doing.

Eva: After getting quite a few bids and spending some time comparing them, she decided to go with the more expensive inset white cabinets with furniture feet. She feels that the money will be well spent and she's thrilled to be getting a pantry too. She picked the cabinetmaker that was higher but spent the most time with her and who had a thorough bid. His cabinets will take longer to make but she felt the quality was higher and she believed that he could deliver what he promised. She felt confident this was a good choice.

The soft-closing drawers cost extra money too, but they were worth it. After looking around she found a good stove that allowed her to remove the wall oven and just have a freestanding stove, giving her space for a pantry. Since she isn't buying any other appliances, she will able to redo her lights and have all new outlets installed to really modernize her kitchen. Plus she will be able to add a refrigerator cabinet to make her appliance blend in and provide additional storage above. After all of her research and time, she felt much more prepared for this project.

Eva's Kitchen Budget

	PROPOSED	ACTUAL
Demo	$650	$750
Cabinetry	$9,700	$11,300
Countertops	$4,300	$4,600
Flooring	0	0
Appliances (stove)	$2,000	$2,015
Tile	$1,500	$1,523
Electrical	$1,400	$1,850
Plumbing	$1,200	$1,100
TOTAL BUDGET	$20,750	$23,138

Eva (cont.)

Moving Forward: Eva has looked over her final budget and decided that, because she has the time, flexibility, and a clear vision of what she wants, she will hire the individual contractors herself. She's a little nervous, but feels pretty comfortable with the quality people that bid the job. Now she just has to figure out how to put a plan in place and pick a start date!

Elaine

Elaine: They decided to choose a slightly less-expensive door style since they had so many cabinets and she wanted all the extra drawers. Her budget for large handles was more than she expected but she's thrilled about the refrigerator cabinet and they were able to find a Wolf stove that they both love.

Elaine's Kitchen Budget

	PROPOSED	ACTUAL
Cabinetry	$9,700	$12,300
Countertops	$4,300	$5,100
Flooring	$9,850	$7,600
Appliances	$7,000	$7,000
Tile	$1,500	$1,623
Electrical	$1,650	$3,000
Plumbing	$1,500	$2,500
General Contractor		$7,825
TOTAL BUDGET	$35,500	$46,948

Moving Forward: After a lot of soul-searching and looking at lots of bids, they found that many of the items they wanted cost a bit more than their original budget. With time quickly slipping away, they were under the gun. They needed to decide whether to postpone the job until the following year, or make decisions immediately and get started.

To save on expenses, they compromised on a lovely cabinet. It had less fancy detail but it was still very well built. They also decided to go with a less expensive flooring option since it was just a neutral color and not their main emphasis. They ended up finding the exact stove they both loved and decided that the investment for them was worth it. Finally, they found a great general contractor that they both liked who could make the project happen within their time frame—if they moved forward right away. Now they just need to decide to pull the trigger.

Implementing Your Plan
Turning Your Dream Into Reality

So you've finally reached this step! You understand how to create a kitchen that functions well, your storyboard is complete, you've done your research, priced things out, and made a budget. Now comes the fun part: making it happen. This next section covers a lot of ground and is the final step in starting your remodel. If you've made it this far, you are better prepared than most people when the dust starts to fly.

I've broken this section down into manageable parts so you know just what to expect. I've included how to set realistic expectations, hiring your contractors, what a basic plan should look like, the natural order of the process, and how long things generally take. These are the topics I talk about the most with my own clients.

Setting Expectations

Taking this first step and setting realistic expectations will go a long way towards preparing you for the journey you are about to take. There are three concepts that I help my clients with to prepare them. Understanding the emotional impact, making sure your expectations are realistic, and creating a clear plan. If you pay attention to these three concepts, you will be prepared and feel a sense of control and confidence.

So let's be honest, doing a major remodel has an enormous emotional impact. There is just no way around this. Anyone who tells you differently is just trying to pretend that it's not going to happen.

The truth is that a remodel is a marathon not a sprint. If you know it's a marathon, you can pace yourself. You save your energy for the really big problems. You know what's on the road ahead and you can plan for the large hills. So when something happens, such as finding additional problems that must be fixed, or someone drops the ball, it's not the end of the world. We just assess the problem, fix it, and move on. Clients who have unrealistic expectations and think they can "make" things happen through sheer force of will are not going to enjoy their experience and will make things much worse than they need to be.

Accept your new reality. Accept that you will have strangers coming in and out of your house. Dust, dirt, extreme noise, tools, materials, chaos, and problems will permeate your home. You will have to be available to make decisions and respond to questions and situations for a period of time.

Set up a small temporary kitchen in another space where you can have your toaster, coffee pot, snacks, plates, and silverware. Create a new strategy to use this limited kitchen while work is being done on the old one. Realize that your life will be like this for a time. Do not imagine that it's just going to be a few days and then suddenly get upset when work goes on longer than you expected. This will just add to your frustration. Your ability to be an effective *manager* of this project will be negatively affected if you are constantly annoyed with the pace of the project.

BUT keep in mind that this project will last a finite period. If you've made good contractor selections (so you know you're in capable hands), then as long as there is consistent progress, you know you will get through it. Accept that you will be uncomfortable for a period of time, but it will end.

You would be shocked to know how many people move forward without thinking through the basic steps for a remodel. There are a lot of logistics that go into managing all the contractors, access, money, etc.

Don't figure you can just wing it! If you try to figure it out as you go, it's nearly impossible for everyone else to know what the plan is. Think through the plan and make sure you have discussed it with your general contractor if you're using one. If you are in charge, know what you are going to do. Make a plan and make sure it is realistic.

Nothing is more stressful than not knowing where you are in the process and why it's taking so long. If you already have a basic idea of each stage and what's reasonable, you will be better prepared and able to manage your stress level.

For instance, if the cabinetmaker tells you that all of the cabinets will be installed in two days but everyone else says it will take two weeks, then your spidey sense should be on high alert. One of two things is about to occur: either he will totally miss his deadline not caring about your schedule and having to move everyone else around OR he will do it in two days and the quality will be horrible. And then you will end up fixing and trying to redo what should have been done correctly the first time.

Most problems occur because the industry is known for not wanting to be honest with homeowners about timing and expectations. They would rather tell you what you want to hear and then quickly get the job done. *Make sure you have created a clear plan* and have attached *realistic time expectations* based on talking to multiple vendors.

Remember that your storyboard is your friend! Be sure everyone sees it and gets on the same page. Have detailed drawings of all cabinetry, samples of all colors, and guidelines which indicate how they should appear when finished.

Creating Your Plan

Whether you decide to manage the project yourself or hire a professional, you still need to have a basic plan to get it done. Below are the steps, including steps we've already covered, to creating a plan everyone can follow.

1. Design storyboard

2. Get bids (based on wish list)

   + check licenses

   + check referrals

   + check bonds

   + check homeowners' insurance

   + check permits

3. Readjust storyboard (based on bids and budget)

4. Hire main contractors

   + create tentative schedule (based on longest lead time)

   + purchase longest-lead-time item (cabinets)

   + purchase or sign contracts (second-largest lead time)

5. Determine start date

   + demo

   + permits

   + access

   + set up temporary accommodations for pets and kids

   + prepare staging area

   + determine where to put your stuff during construction

6. Day 1: start of the "REAL" work

Hiring Contractors

I often tell my clients that starting a full kitchen remodel is like pregnancy. In the beginning, you're super-excited and all you can see is cute baby clothes and all the lovely bits of the adventure. In the middle, you start to realize just how big of an endeavor it's going to be and you start to freak out a bit. Before you know it you are eight months pregnant, fat, you can't reach your feet to tie your shoes, and you're pissed off at everyone! You just want it to be over, but then . . . the baby is born and all you can see is how beautiful she is and how happy she makes you, and you forget all about the struggle and misery you went through.

Nobody ever believes me when I share that story. And this is on jobs where everything goes well. But by the end, the feelings are similar. You are tired of the mess and making decisions all the time and dealing with people in your house—even if you like them! So the bottom line is that just like pregnancy, a kitchen remodel is a marathon with a fantastic ending. If you look at it like that, you will not be disappointed and you'll forget all about how annoyed you were when you hold your beautiful new kitchen in your arms.

Whether you've decided to manage hiring everyone yourself or will use a general contractor, there are still some basic measures you should take to protect yourself. They involve the hiring process, job site management, and quality control.

 # Hiring Process

I stress the word **process** because its takes a lot of time to get detailed bids, compare them, and check referrals and licenses. So give yourself the time to be thorough. That said, do not presume that you have all the time in the world to do this. Exceptional contractors have full schedules all the time for a reason. Be respectful of their time, and call them to confirm. When you call them promptly and provide them with what they need in a timely fashion, they will work to fit you into their schedule. If you wait until it's convenient for you, nine out of ten times, they will not take your job because they've booked other clients. Then you will have to start all over again, usually with a lesser-quality contractor.

Let's delve a little further into how you can protect yourself by choosing qualified professionals.

Hiring a General Contractor

Remember that this person will determine how people work in your home—how neat, how safe, the schedule, the day-to-day timing, and quality control. You really want someone you feel comfortable with handling things and fixing problems. Do not just choose the flashy guy who is funny and talks a good game. Think of it like dating. This person is going to be a big part of your life for weeks or months.

You want someone with intimate knowledge of the timing, the materials, and the quality of the work being done. Otherwise, in my opinion, it's a waste of money to hire a general contractor if you could do the job yourself just as well. In addition to his or her professional qualifications and licenses, I also look for the following traits in a general contractor.

Responsiveness

Since this is the person who will have the most contact with you and everyone else, you definitely want someone who answers their phone, returns phone calls and texts, and who is open to contact and discussion. The old traditional guys that never return calls and hate to discuss design or how things are going should be out the door. Do not accept this behavior.

Receptiveness

You do not want someone who is arrogant and treats you like you are too dumb to understand anything. Just because you are not familiar with the work at a professional level is not a reason for a tradesperson to be condescending. You want someone who is willing to educate you. Also remember that you want someone who, if problems arise, you would feel comfortable confronting and have confidence that they'd work hard to get the problem fixed.

Compatible Work Habits

It is important that you align yourself with someone who shares your values or will blend in with your basic lifestyle. If you and your husband both work nights and you need to sleep all day, obviously you will need to work with someone who will figure out a schedule that you can stick to. If you are a stay-at-home mom, you need to work with someone who understands the chaos and you can both work out a schedule to get things done. If you hire someone who is never on time and never returns phone calls, and you are stickler for that then you will have a miserable time throughout the entire remodel. Be clear up front what your typical schedule is and pick someone who can stick to a timetable that keeps the project moving forward.

Hire for Personality

When you hire people you enjoy and believe in, they will be an emotional buffer to the chaos that is any remodel. They will help pull you through. They will listen and care about your concerns. When issues arise, they will quickly and easily fix them and maintain progress. *They will CARE about disappointing you and will act accordingly.* Ultimately you are paying people for services and products, but in my experience nothing can protect you from people that do not care about your job. Look for people that show an interest in you and your needs and *want* to satisfy you.

NOTE: Do not choose based on who has the lowest price. Use your intuition, think hard about who you believe has your best interests at heart, who is REALLY listening to you, and shares your vision. That person will do a better job, no matter the price of his or her bid. The worst decision you can make is to hire someone who does not respect you. It will not matter how "successful" that company is or how well respected, that contractor will do the absolute bare minimum on your job and you will be constantly frustrated.

Hire for Character

There are lots of contractors out there that will seek to take advantage of your ignorance. Being forewarned is being forearmed. Hire someone you trust. Women, this means using your intuition. Do not underestimate the importance of this! You still need to do all the "regular" things you would do to check the legality and legitimacy of your contractor, but there is no substitute for trusting someone. Do not hire someone you would not trust in your house or who you feel does not respect you.

Special Considerations when Hiring Electricians

In my experience, an electrician who takes the time to install outlets correctly is usually the same guy that takes the time to do the electrical work correctly *behind* the walls that you don't see. It is the stuff behind the walls that can cause house fires, endangering your family and risking your personal belongings. If you see visible clues of shoddy work, you should be worried. The quality and experience level of the electrician is often directly related to his or her finish work.

A good electrician will consider the cabinets when determining the position of your recessed lighting and will ask for your participation in determining correct positioning of all light fixtures and switches. Time and attention should be spent figuring out how you want to control your lights, if they are dimmable, how many switches, and the look of all cover plates.

He or she will also be neat and clean, typically. A messy electrician is a warning sign that he or she does not have the necessary attention to detail and you want this quality in an electrician especially. *You do not want someone that cuts corners in this trade*. So when considering which electrician to hire, take your time, ask questions, and choose wisely.

 ## Protect Yourself

In order to protect yourself there are some things that state agencies have created to help with sifting through good and bad contractors. I will explain what each means and how they are intended to work but I want to emphasize that none of these will stop a dishonest contractor. It might be possible to get restitution from one of those agencies for an unscrupulous contractor, but it will take a long time and be an enormous hassle. The goal is to *avoid* lousy contractors if at all possible.

Permits

With virtually all kitchen remodels, city permits are necessary. One remodel may in fact require numerous permits, customized for your particular project. Each city has different standards and requirements. You must get a permit from your city development office, usually the city planning department. You will bring in plans to show what changes you will be making and they will assess a fee based on a percentage. Then as your work progresses, an inspector will visit the job site and sign off to ensure that it meets city building codes. Be warned that issues of quality control are not considered in this process, so you must do your own quality control. If you are hiring a general contractor, often he will "pull" the permit. This is a good idea to ensure that a licensed professional is on the job.

Licenses

Not every state requires licensing, so if your state does not, things will be even more difficult if you run into a problem. This makes double-checking the contractors' references even more important.

If your state *does* require licensing like in California, which has some of the most stringent requirements, this discussion is for you. Agencies that issue licenses require that contractors submit their qualifications, including years on the job, and take a written test to show basic understanding of their field. These requirements vary widely from state to state. In addition, even states like California that have extremely strict requirements *do not assess actual quality of work or real competence.*

So just because a contractor is licensed in a certain field is no guarantee that his quality of work is high.

In the state of California, licensed contractors must also be bonded. The bond is an amount of money held in trust. If you have reason to file a claim for nonperformance, you file the claim with the license office which acts on your behalf and pursues the contractor. In California, the bond is $12,500. However, the contractor is given first right to fix or finish the job. If he refuses, the bond money is sent to the consumer.

However, it is not as simple as just calling them up and saying that you are unhappy. It is a long and involved process and you have to prove you were harmed. Oh and by the way, meanwhile your job is at a complete standstill. You do not want to go through this process; so choose your contractor carefully in the beginning.

Use State Agencies

Go to Google.com, type in your state's name and "contractor license." This should bring up the agency that is in charge of licensing and provide the website where you can search by license number. Once there, make sure to pay attention to any claims or grievances listed under that contractor. Additionally, call that agency and ask what the bond requirements are for the specific trade you are hiring and ask how to check to make sure it is up to date.

Homeowners' Insurance

Another step you should take before you have any workmen on your property is to check with your homeowners' insurance policy. Find out what is covered and what isn't if someone gets hurt on your property. Discuss any shortfalls and coverage with your contractors *before* work starts.

Additional Research

This website provides a good overview of the process and things to consider when hiring a contractor:

http://www.angieslist.com/contractor/license-bonded-insured.htm

When the references have checked out, you've done your due diligence, and you have decided whom you will hire, call the contractor(s), let them know they were selected, and find out what they need from you to secure your place on their schedule.

 ## Signing Contracts

Once you are ready to sign contracts, remember that if it's not written down clearly, it isn't legal and enforceable. Make sure all the major contracts you sign are easy for you to understand, have clear details about what is and isn't included in the scope of work, and have two other important clauses—a payment schedule based on progress and results, and an exit strategy.

 ## Progress Payments

One of the biggest mistakes I see women make when dealing with contractors is failing to have a clear plan regarding payments. The larger the bid, the more details there will be, and so the more spread out the payments should be. Most, if not all, contractors will require some sort of deposit, especially if large amounts of materials need to be ordered. This is normal. At some point, once items start being delivered and installed, additional payments must be made. For example, at our shop we break down cabinetry into four payments: a material deposit, a progress payment, and two installation payments. Not every contractor is going to want to do that, but just bear in mind that a lot can happen from the beginning of the job to the end. You will want to have some control by tying payments to performance.

 ## Exit Strategy

Sometimes a customer gets stuck with someone they no longer want to work with. It happens. And I understand how. In the beginning they are so excited to get started, and they "just want one person that can handle it all!" How many times have I heard that? So they sign up with one person who is supposed to handle all aspects of the work. Let's go even further and say that this homeowner didn't follow any of my other advice either and just hired the first person with the lowest price. They didn't care that this person didn't seem that interested in the project, and, frankly, now they're not really interested in him either. *They just want the job done.*

But here's the problem, in every project there will be things that have to be worked out. There will be things that were unplanned and need to be fixed before moving on. There is an eighty percent chance that items *will* cost more than expected, things will take longer than anticipated, and frustration will occur!

That is why it is so important to work with someone you like, that you trust, and who will help you navigate these obstacles and keep moving. If not, you will be in a world of hurt.

If you're the unfortunate homeowner who ignored my advice, then there could be consequences. That contractor (who at the time you didn't like, but you thought it didn't matter) becomes the person you most want to avoid and can't seem to communicate with. The problems will escalate since neither of you has much respect for the other. And since you signed a contract for ALL of it, what can you do? Sue him? Hire another contractor? Stop the project?

All of those things cost a lot more money and meanwhile you're sitting with a gutted kitchen, with no running water, and nowhere to turn. If you think that can't happen to you, think again. It happens all the time. So here are my suggestions.

First, create an exit strategy or build in some sort of performance aspect to your job. Think ahead and find a way out in case you need it. Second, try to keep some of the aspects of the remodel separate. For instance, when we bid jobs, we never do a total number. We bid on multiple aspects of a job separately. We feel strongly that if we bid them together and the customer is unhappy with our cabinets, why should they be forced to continue working with us for countertop fabrication?

So we give a bid for cabinets, a bid for countertops, and a bid for flooring if required. Along the way, we're often asked to add in plumbing and electrical, but each is still separate. That way at any point, if they aren't happy, they can continue the project using other contractors. It's just something to think about.

I understand how it might be hard to untangle the different skills and job tasks. Give it some thought and always have an exit strategy and a way for work to continue just in case the quality or performance is so bad you want to exit or discontinue the relationship.

Open Communications

Finally, be sure to maintain consistent (but not pushy) communications. If something is not up to your standard or you are not happy, do not wait until eighty percent of the job is done and then blow up. This will not lead to a satisfactory conclusion.

Instead, start with kind and simple communication, firmly but respectfully said, with clear expectations. This is especially important when something does go wrong. You will be surprised at how quickly most contractors will work to fix the issue with you. Women often have a hard time causing conflict or confronting someone. But if it's done early on and with respect, you will have a much better chance of getting what you want.

The worst thing you can possibly do is wait until the end and then go through a huge list of things you're unhappy about. At that point, it's too hard to fix and it seems to come out of nowhere. I often get complaints from customers about other contractors at the end of their job—that they can't get their problems addressed but they have already paid, so by then it is too late.

Don't be that customer. Communicate early, often, and respectfully.

Details, Details

One of the hardest things for homeowners to understand is the natural order of things to come. They struggle with the timing and understanding how all of the trades fit together. I put together a chart that illustrates the most common trades involved in a kitchen remodel. If you're going to play the role of general contractor, you can review the chart to determine the lead times for each vendor you will hire. You must work backwards to create a tentative schedule. For instance, custom cabinets typically take six to eight weeks for production *after* the design process is completed, then installation takes two weeks. Tile and specialty items or appliances often have two to three weeks of lead time.

Natural Order of Things in Detail

STEP	STAGES OF CONSTRUCTION	TIME DURATION	DETAILS
1	Demolition	1–3 days	
2	Rough framing	1–2 weeks	move/change walls
3	Rough-in plumbing	1–2 days	add/repair
4	Rough-in electrical	1–2 days	add/repair
5	Sheetrock repair/texture	1 week	
6	Paint (neutral ceilings and walls)	1–3 days	
7	Flooring	1–2 weeks	wood or tile
8	Cabinet installation	2 weeks	
9	Template countertops	2 weeks	template, fabricate
10	Appliance installation	1–2 days	
11	Countertop installation	1 day	install
12	Finish plumbing	1–2 days	hookup DW, new sink, fridge, stove
13	Tile (backsplash)	4–5 days	
14	Finish electrical	1–2 days	Final fixtures, cover plates, etc.
15	Final paint (touch up and accent wall)	1–2 days	
	MOVE BACK IN!		

Job Site Management

There are many things that can make or break a kitchen remodel and this is one area that very few contractors ever talk about directly with customers. But I guarantee you they talk about it behind your back. In order to create a good working environment for your own project, I am going to share an insider's view of the most common frustrations that cause conflict and create a *slow work zone*.

A slow work zone is usually the result of contractors feeling frustrated because they can't work efficiently on your job site. So they tend to go to the easiest locations to work first. This is not necessarily intentional, it is basic human nature. Where would you rather work? In an office with screaming people, tons of chaos, where you can barely get to your desk, and are constantly interrupted? Or do you prefer a quiet, easily accessible workspace with no interruptions?

The best job sites are accessible, quiet, and stress-free. This makes it easy for contractors to do their job and focus. Every day we, as contractors, unload massive amounts of tools and materials, often carrying them over long distances, setting up our workspace (or trying to find one), trying to focus on the task at hand and solving problems all day long.

Meanwhile, we are constantly being interrupted, dealing with problems that arise on other jobs, handling phone calls from new customers, dealing with vendors and material delivery. Every single day we deal with this kind of stress and have to find a way to do a beautiful job. When we show up at your house, this becomes our office space. You will get the best out of us if you make it an easy space for us to work in. *This means your job will get done sooner and the quality will be better.* If you've never heard this before it's because no one wants to tell it like it is.

If you are managing the job site, you will want to create a schedule and make it an easy environment for the contractors to work in. To accomplish this I've created a list of distractions to keep out of your work zone *before* everyone gets there. Please don't wait until the last minute or they will be wasting time waiting while you get organized. This will create tension on your site whether you notice it or not.

If you hired a general contractor, this would be part of his job. He would set up the work site so that his workers can get started right away. But you can accomplish the same thing yourself.

Access

- Clear driveway and space for parking **before** workers are set to arrive.
- Create space for working (allow for tools and materials).

- Set up work schedule so you can stay out of their way—this is key.
- Clear path or obstacles so they can easily walk to and from your location.

Distractions

- Don't interrupt their work flow. Save your questions for after work time.
- Keep kids out of the work site.
- Don't allow pets to pester workers.
- Keep TV or radio to a reasonable noise level.
- Get boxes and random stuff out of the work area.
- Keep non-contractor activity and traffic out of the work zone.

Set Up a Temporary Kitchen

- Set up a long table (at least six feet long) in another location.
- Include toaster, coffee, snacks, plates, glasses, cups, and utensils.

Regarding the Schedule

- Be flexible.
- Create set times when everyone knows you will be out of the way so they can work.
- Set weekly, not daily, goals.

 # Quality Control

As a homeowner it can be really difficult to judge whether a job is well done or not. Even those homeowners who are handy and do a lot of do-it-yourself projects aren't educated about the professional industry standards for each trade. It is only when you have professional experience within a trade that you come to understand the differences between a high-quality job and one that's poorly done.

I've compiled a list of some of the things I look for when I am inspecting a job. These qualities will give you some perspective and help you determine the quality of each aspect of your job. I've organized the list by what you should look for within each trade. There is a detailed explanation of each trade within the Quality Control Library at the back of this book.

It should be noted that this is not an exhaustive list and isn't meant to substitute for working with high quality contractors. This is meant to give you some idea of which things are most important to notice *before* you make your final payments.

So now that we've talked about the best way to implement your plan and start construction, let's check in one last time and see how Eva and Elaine did with using this information. I know they spent a lot of time up front qualifying their contractors and really understanding the materials and choices that go into building their custom kitchen cabinets. I hope they enjoyed the process and I am looking forward to hearing about their beautiful new kitchens.

Eva

"I felt a lot more confident about the choices I made and I loved looking at my storyboard! It was stressful and a long process getting bids and doing all the checking of licenses and referrals, but I was able to manage it because my expectations were realistic. I picked people who were really good at their jobs and whom I trusted so I couldn't wait to get started on the project.

I did decide to move the remodel back two months so my schedule would be less stressful since I was the one managing the project. I created my schedule and let all the other contractors know where they fit in. I cleared out old stuff to make room for my temporary kitchen and reminded myself to be flexible.

I'm thrilled that I came in under my budget and I got more than I originally thought possible. After it was over I felt so great about my final choices and I am so in love with my beautiful new kitchen."

Elaine

"What I realize now is just how unprepared we were before. My husband and I thought it would be so quick and easy, I think because we were used to watching kitchen remodels on television. We were really in for a rude awakening. I'm not going to lie and say it was easy going through this process, but we felt so much more prepared. We spent more in several areas and things cost more than we expected but we feel it was within our control so we didn't feel like it 'just happened to us.'

The research and bidding process gave us the confidence to enjoy our choices. Originally we both thought we could easily manage the process and save some money but in the end, after seeing how many people and trades were involved and the timing issue, we just felt that hiring a professional that we trusted would be worth the extra cost. We hired a licensed general contractor to help us manage the process and were confident he would get it done in the time period we had. It really helped to have all those conversations before we started demo.

We found so many things that we didn't know to ask. It was very useful for us to keep our different expectations in check. I can see why so many marriages are tested during this process. When it was over we were so thrilled that our kitchen was done on time and was even more beautiful than we envisioned. We are so glad we picked someone we trusted and who could help us navigate those rough patches."

Section 9

Your Story's Happy Ending

We've come a long way together, you and I. We've explored the importance of DFIO, discovered the tips and tricks of working with contractors, and you've probably learned more about cabinets, countertops, and appliances than you ever dreamed of. I hope I've impressed upon you the need for a plan, a storyboard, and a budget. The time you spend qualifying contractors and getting ready to start the remodel will pay off in the end with a kitchen you'll truly fall in love with.

I sincerely hope that this book has made the journey easier for you. I hope that, because you followed its advice, you're sitting in your beautiful dream kitchen right now. You know where everything is stored and you know that you'll never have to empty out an entire cabinet to find something again.

It's an emotional ride, but the ending is the best part. Now, you too have a kitchen you can fall in love with, full of DFIO-focused features like Blum soft-closing slides, banks of drawers, and garbage pull-outs. Who knew garbage could make such a difference in a kitchen?

My customers are always skeptical at first that these features can really make such a big difference in their kitchen, but by the end of their remodel they are completely in love with their new kitchens. So in love, in fact, that some have even written love letters to their kitchens. Keep reading for a peek at a few of these love letters, and be sure to send me your own kitchen love story when you're finished!

Warmly,

Camille

Dear Kitchen,

I love you, simple as that. You have made my life better and I could not be happier with our newfound relationship. I wasn't happy in our previous relationship; you were old, unattractive, and dysfunctional. It was embarrassing to introduce you to my friends and family, but now people cannot get enough of you, including myself.

It used to be a nightmare to prepare dinner or even get a cup of coffee in the mornings with you, but now you make my life so easy and you also happen to be a dream to look at every day. I never thought I would be excited about your trash can, but sure enough, I am. It is hidden and out of the way so no one can see it or smell it. It has its own sliding cabinet, which makes food preparation so much easier and just hanging out so much more comfortable. Your cabinets are stunning, and the luxurious soft-closing feature allows for a quiet morning of just me, you and a cup of coffee. Your beautiful cabinets have given me so much space to work with, that I am now able to stay organized, and cook and entertain with ease.

I couldn't imagine my life without you now. I am so thankful that Camille was able to introduce us and help create our extraordinary relationship. You make me happy and I enjoy entertaining and showing you off to my friends and family. I am so excited to continue our life together and create delicious food and lasting memories.

> With love,
> Michelle Trippi

Dear Kitchen,

I knew I was ready for a change. Your cabinets were outdated and dark. Your version of "organization" had run amuck. Your countertops were keeping me from another love—baking. I knew it was time to reassess our relationship. It was time for me to be free. Free from grout, free from the darkness of your cabinets . . . the truth is, I wanted to be free from you.

But, then I met Camille, who is truly a kitchen matchmaker. We put the plan in motion to reface the cabinets, update lower cabinets with drawers, and replace existing lighting. And now, I love you!

Your transformation was amazing. You are not only beautiful but you're also organized and functional. At the time of the reface, I just wanted you to look pretty, but with Camille's expertise we went from disorganized cabinets and make-shift home office with cluttered drawers to efficiency in every area. Installation of the drawers for pots and pans, Tupperware-type items, and spice drawer with each and every spice at my fingertips made my kitchen a dream to work in. Recessed can lighting and beautiful white cabinets have made my dark kitchen come to life. Amazingly gorgeous "Earth Glitter" granite countertops backed by a tile backsplash leave you lost in the beauty of the movement of the granite. I want to spend so much time with you because you've become a beautiful haven. I am so grateful to Camille, owner of Divine Kitchen, for making my dreams come true. I know we will thoroughly enjoy our retirement years together.

Love,
Darlene Conner

Dear Kitchen,

Don't take this personally, but we didn't like you. You were old and worn out, poorly made, cheap, and dysfunctional. But now, we can't get enough of you—we love you.

Getting a cup of coffee, making lunch, or just congregating for conversation was a daunting task, but now we are able to enjoy and embrace every efficient characteristic of you. Your cabinet and drawers were loud and out of date, and might I add, very unattractive. It was impossible to open and close drawers to grab utensils or pots and pans because of your peculiar layout. After much debate, we finally chose different cabinets, new drawers, and the right decorative hardware to turn you into our dream kitchen. With soft-closing drawers and specific cabinets for pots and pans, you are incredibly functional and a dream to cook in.

Looking back, I don't know how we ever lived without you. You are a perfect match. We are so thankful that Camille was able to introduce us to you. She truly listened to everything we needed and preferred in a kitchen, and she produced an incredible match for us. We look forward to cooking and entertaining now, and without her help, that would have never been possible.

> With Much Love,
> Rex and Jenny Barr

Dear Kitchen,

When we first saw you, we knew it was love at first sight. Before your transformation, it was obvious that our relationship with you was over a long time ago. Things were just too complicated; the cabinets didn't fit our pots and pans, the appliances were out of date, and it was impossible to host a family dinner. But now, you are beautifully functional and we love you unconditionally.

It was the little things that helped us fall in love with you all over again. The beautiful granite countertops, the impeccably crafted cabinets, and the customized hood over the stove helped rekindle the love in our relationship. Your customized cabinets that were specifically made for our pots and pans and the handy spice rack located right next to the stove that makes adding a splash of flavor to any dish easier than ever, has made cooking and entertaining a dream again.

Camille was the perfect matchmaker; we should call her cupid. She listened to every quality we look for in a partner and she was able to produce the perfect match. Camille understood exactly what we were looking for and we were able to put our trust in her, and we are glad we did. Without you, we wouldn't be able to host our family dinners again when the kids come home for the weekend. We are able to converse and cook with ease, and we love you for that.

> Love always,
> Patti and Ryan Bales

Reference Library

On most jobs, my clients tend to have the same questions and concerns. One of the things they struggle with is the volume of unfamiliar terminology involved when you remodel a kitchen. They have lots of questions about "what" something is, about "how" something works, and "why" certain things are the way they are. On top of that I find that very few people know how to gauge the quality of the work being done in their homes or in the materials they purchase. I created the Reference Library and the Quality Control Library to explain some of these concepts in greater detail.

The Reference Library will help explain what common terms in construction mean. I feel that these are the most important terms for you to understand. I have also included my perspective as needed, based on what I see on job sites every day. This library is intended to educate you and prevent you from making a bad choice.

Cabinetry

This is a major investment, so you should take your time and consider the overall style of the door (which contributes significantly to the design of the kitchen) and the color of the kitchen cabinets, along with the quality of the cabinets. *Quality* of cabinets can be confusing for the average homeowner because it is made up of so many components. I've broken down cabinetry into seven sections: cabinet box, cabinet face frame, cabinet door, cabinet drawer box, drawer front, hardware and finish.

For examples of each section, visit *www.divinekitchen.net/cabinetry*.

Cabinet Box

The cabinet "box," also known in the industry as the "case," is the five-sided box that is attached in the back to your wall. It is where you are actually set your items. It's what your shelves are attached to and is a critical, but very often-overlooked part of your cabinet. The "face frame" is attached directly to this box and is the part you see when facing your cabinets. You might want to look at your current cabinet to see if you can determine where the face frame joins with the "box."

The most important aspect of choosing cabinets is to make sure the box is made of ¾″ cabinet-grade material. Lower-end shops will use ½″ sides and shelves. Wood that is only a ½″ thick will warp and bend, and some "less-than-honest" builders will charge the same as for ¾″ material. Obviously, try to avoid these cabinet shops.

The box is important because it is the structure to which everything else is attached. The face frame is attached to the box, then the door is attached to the side of the box or face frame, the walls of the box are used to support the shelves, etc. If you choose a cabinet box that is made of cheap material, everything else will be compromised.

Cabinet Face Frame

Kitchen cabinets come in several styles, but probably the most misunderstood are how the fronts are finished. For many years there were only two styles, both of which were called face-frame cabinets. The face frame is the hardwood frame that determines the openings where a door or a drawer goes. That "frame" would then be attached to the "box" and then the doors and drawers would be attached to that entire assembly.

Those two styles of face frames are called "overlay" and "inset." What makes this complicated is that in the past twenty years the cabinet industry has introduced another style called "frameless."

Overlay

Overlay is when the doors sit "outside" or overlay on top of the frame on all four sides. It is the most standard type and the least expensive. It is the style of the majority of cabinetry.

Inset

This is when the doors and drawer fronts are made to fit "inside" the actual face frame. There is typically a thin space on all sides of the door and drawer front enabling it room to move. In magazines you will often see this look with a small bead or groove around each opening. These cabinets are very often white or painted an opaque color where no grain or wood shows through.

This is typically the most expensive type of "face frame" cabinet to build, because of the time and experience required. I feel that the difference is worth the price. If you are looking for pretty and stylish, this type of cabinet instantly creates a dramatic look.

Frameless (also known as European)

This style of cabinet is made with the same ¾" material for the box but has no hardwood face frame attached. The front "rough" face is edge banded with matching material. Then the doors and drawers are attached. It is the most standard type of cabinet produced in Europe and has become very popular in the US. In a frameless cabinet, the doors and drawer fronts *always* cover most of the visible box of the cabinet. Think of modern or Ikea-style cabinetry.

Cabinet Door/Drawer Front

There are many, many door styles but I am only going to cover the *four* most common concepts, so as not to overwhelm you with information. When you shop for cabinets you will decide between the style of door (typically solid plank, raised panel or recessed panel) and you will need to decide the way that the doors are made (typically using butt or miter joints).

Doors

Doors come in all types of woods and construction but perhaps the most important thing to know is the difference between a five-piece solid-panel door and a ¼″ recessed-panel door. The recessed panel door is extremely popular and is best known for the Shaker-style door in white seen in so many magazines. Women just love it! However, it is a really cheap door and will bend and twist since there is very little hardwood in the middle to hold it stable.

A five-piece door and drawer front refers to the way it is made—using five pieces. Four outside pieces create the frame and the inside panel is the fifth piece. I prefer a five-piece solid-panel door and drawer front. A five-piece solid-panel door has a ¾″ solid wood middle, eliminating the hollow sound. It creates a much more stable door which will resist warping and twisting.

If you want the look of a white Shaker door but you don't want it to warp like the cheaper version, you can accomplish this by using a simple five-piece door with a flat ⅜″ solid hardwood panel or a five-piece door with a simplified no detail ¾″ solid panel. Make sure there is no detail anywhere else on the door and you will have a sleek but solid Shaker style that will resist warping and twisting.

Drawer Front

This is the small panel or "front" that goes on the drawer box. Most people assume that the drawer is all one piece, but actually it is made up of two pieces, the box and the front. Lower-end shops may use a solid single piece for the front with no design elements to save money. But it is worth the small upgrade to a use a five-piece drawer front that matches your door. It adds strength and a lot to the overall "custom" look of your new kitchen.

Raised Panel

This is a solid ¾″ panel that is used for the middle of the door, creating rigidity and strength. The "raised" part refers to the middle section that comes out towards you and appears raised up from the door.

Recessed panel

This is a ¼″ panel used for the middle of the door which creates a "recessed" look in the middle of the door. It is very popular with Shaker-style doors. This is a very clean and minimal look, but the downside is that the door has a tendency to warp over time because of the thinness of the panel in the middle of the door. It also has a hollow sound if you knock on the middle of the doors, which is especially noticeable in doors larger than 30″ tall.

Door Joints

All doors are made using one of *two* types of joints—miter joints or butt joints. The stronger of the two joints is the butt joint, which is the least likely to move over time. However, all doors that are made of wood expand and contract subtly over time. This is natural. The upside of choosing a butt joint door is that, if you are doing a painted finish, you will minimize (but not eliminate) visible cracks over time. The downside is that this type of joint severely limits your possible design styles, because many can only be made with a miter joint.

Butt Joint

A door is created with square or abutting edges. This joint is the strongest and resists cracking and movement the best. However, some popular styles can't be made with butt joints.

Miter Joint

In this construction, the corners of the door are angled or mitered at 45° in the corners. This joint has a greater possibility of developing a thin gap or line after a period of drying, but it does offer you the possibility of some beautiful door styles that can't be made in a butt joint. Usually, miter joints can be filled with matching wood filler if they open slightly over the years.

Cabinet Drawer Box

A drawer box is the actual five-sided box or structure into which you place items like pots, zip-top bags, utensils, etc. It is made with four strips of wood joined at the corners with a bottom inserted. There is a wide range of styles and choices, and cost varies widely. However there are typically *two* major types of construction and *two* common materials used for most cabinet drawers.

Dovetail Drawer Box

A dovetail drawer box refers to the type of corner construction where "dovetails" of interlocking wood are joined creating the strongest corner.

Square Joint

This type of drawer box joint is used on economy drawer boxes and refers to overlapping edges at the corners. It is weaker than a dovetail joint since the wood isn't interwoven on all corners. If correctly made, this is a perfectly acceptable lower-cost option.

White Melamine Drawer Boxes

This is probably the most common type of economy material. It's used for most kitchen drawer boxes today. It cleans easily and makes the inside of your drawer boxes bright.

Wood Drawer Boxes

Drawer boxes made of wood come in two types: solid and plywood. These are most often made from birch, maple, or cherry. You can get the boxes made in either solid hardwood or cabinet grade ½″ plywood. I feel that solid hardwood is highly over-rated and they are significantly more expensive. I do feel a drawer box made of maple or birch ½″ prefinished plywood is well worth the small additional cost over melamine drawer boxes. It's worth it because the insides of the drawers are beautiful and easy to clean, and it just doesn't cost that much more. Our *preferred drawer box* is prefinished birch with a dovetail joint construction used with a Blum soft-closing slide.

Hardware

Because the hardware in your kitchen is what really operates your cabinets and creates a sense of ease and function, to me it is the most important item you can select to create a feel of luxury and enjoyment. When I refer to hardware I'm talking about the slides that move your drawers in and out, the hinges that allow your doors to open and shut, and the handles that you touch every day. *Hardware is your cabinet's internal engine!*

Door Hinges

This is the mechanism that swings the kitchen door shut. These range widely in quality and function. Vast improvements have been made to hinges that allow for greater functionality and ease of use. However, most kitchen cabinets are still installed with cheap hinges that function terribly. It is always a shock to me when I see even high-end cabinets with cheap, imitation hinges. What a tragedy.

My favorite company to use is called Blum. They are made in the US and are by far the best hinge on the market. It only costs a few hundred dollars to put the top-of-the-line Blum soft-closing hinges on your doors. This alone is the one mandatory element that I feel should be in every kitchen, no exceptions.

Be aware that customers are routinely deceived by having their hinges switched to a cheap imitation. It happens all the time in the industry. Authentic Blum hinges have the name "blum" stamped right in the metal. Don't get ripped off! Be sure to look for this stamp on your hinges. To view their site and get additional information go to *www.blum.com.*

European Concealed Hinges

This type of hinge is bored into the backside of the doors using a 35mm bit. This is considered a modern hinge and should be standard on all custom kitchen jobs. When the door is closed you cannot see the hinge or base plate. European concealed hinges are a much stronger hinge than traditional or "visible" hinges.

Drawer Slides

Slides are what operate your drawers. They can either open and close easily or you can fight with them every day. Since you will be using your drawers multiple times daily, they are an integral part of what can make your kitchen a joy to use. The quality and function of slides can vary widely. On the low end there are cheap plastic roller slides that don't pull out all the way (¾ extension). On the high end there are slides that pull all the way out (full extension) and glide back easily (soft closing). I use only Blum soft-closing full-extension slides. This is because they have a 100 lb. rating and they are soft closing so you can literally use your knee to gently shut them. In addition, you want to be able to see and use 100% of your base cabinet, so full extension slides are a must.

Remember slides are the workhorse of your kitchen and attention to this component will greatly improve your enjoyment of your kitchen.

Full Extension

This type of drawer slide extends fully, enabling you to maximize storage for that drawer box. In older homes it was standard to use three-quarter extension drawer slides, that's why it was difficult to get to the back of drawers.

Soft-Close Mechanisms

This is the mechanism that allows door hinges and drawer slides to softly close when shut. The weight of the door or drawer activates the mechanism. You simply push the door or drawer shut, and the soft-close mechanism prevents it from slamming.

 # Finishes

This is the topic women want to talk about the most, the color of the new cabinets. I understand why; they are sick of what they have and want a dramatic change. For 85% of the market that means white cabinets. This is still women's favorite kitchen color. The quality of materials and actual finishing skills range dramatically across the US. This chapter will provide you with some basic definitions so you can hold an intelligent conversation with your cabinetmaker.

You should research what is considered the highest-quality finish in *your* specific area. For instance, in California most high-end custom cabinets are sprayed with conversion varnish or at least a very high-grade pre-catalyzed lacquer. Usually we only see painted (enamel) finishes in extremely expensive homes where they are finished in place by very experienced professional painters. Typically in California when a kitchen is painted with actual paint, these jobs are poorly done by inexperienced finishers. So be wary of paint. It needs to be applied by a very experienced painter to get a professional look and proper protection. Climate often dictates the materials used in an area as well. It is usually dry and warm here most of the year, so we don't have moisture issues like on the East Coast where painting is more common.

Regardless of your location, it is very important to know that your cabinets should never be hand painted. They should only be sprayed in a professional booth. This is the only way to apply a consistent look and even coverage. This applies to stains as well. Spraying is the only way to get even, consistent coverage and control the saturation of the stain.

You should also know that no finish, regardless of what anyone tells will resist constant touching, food, and acids eating into its surface over time. Higher quality finishes like conversion varnish are much more water-resistant, but nothing is impervious. That is why you need good-quality, *large* pulls and knobs—so that you are not constantly touching your cabinets every day. This alone will do a lot to save your finish.

Finally, be aware that most companies charge outrageous markups on popular finishes. While it does take longer to create certain looks, like glazed finishes and some specialty finishes, I feel the industry has done a disservice to the finishing industry by charging extremely high rates. I suspect they charge outrageous amounts for them because they know women want them.

In our shop, we charge a proportional amount for the extra time it takes to create shabby-chic glazes and specialty fatigue finishes. We want our customers to get the look they want without the finish being a determining factor in the overall job price. We do not charge more simply because we know we can due to high demand.

The two terms you will hear the most and that you need to understand are stain grade and paint grade. The two most popular applied finishes are lacquers and conversion varnish.

Stain Grade

This refers to any stain ranging from very light to very dark and everything in between. It simply means a stain is applied (never by hand) and then a clear lacquer or topcoat is applied. Generally it means you can still see the grain of the wood through the stain. For instance let's say you order a birch cabinet with a mocha stain. That is considered a stain-grade cabinet. After stain is applied (for color), it will then have several coats of clear lacquer or conversion varnish applied for protection.

Paint Grade

Contrary to how this sounds, we're not talking about actual paint. "Paint grade" just means that the end result will be opaque. Meaning you will not be able to see *any* grain through the color. So for instance, any white cabinet, whether finished with actual paint (enamel or oil-based paint) or pigmented lacquer or conversion varnish will all be called "paint grade" in the industry. We call it paint grade to refer to the type of wood being used to create a "mirror" finish. We must use a closed grain (maple) instead of an open grain (oak) so that when the finish is applied we get a smooth finished look like in the magazines.

Glazes

This refers to a group of materials that is typically hand applied to the door to give it extra depth, an aged effect, or highlights. Glaze colors include white, grey, dark brown, and black. Van Dyke brown is probably the most common glaze used to create the very popular shabby-chic look seen in most magazines today. When applied over a soft white base, it creates a vintage look. What's important to remember is that it is hand applied and then wiped off to create the distressed look. Because of this, it needs to be done by a very experienced finisher. It takes years of practice to get the "right touch" to create a consistent professional look from door to door. If you choose to have a distressed look, the level of distress can range from messy to clean, so be sure to get an exact door sample of the finish so you can specify how much glaze and/or distressed look you like.

Lacquers

These are the clear topcoat that is applied over the stain (color) you chose. The quality ranges dramatically so spend some time talking with your cabinetmaker to verify what you have chosen is a good-quality finish. This will typically be a lower cost finish compared to conversion varnish. Lacquers are typically less water-resistant than conversion varnish finishes, however lacquers are much easier to repair.

Conversion Varnish

This finish is considered a much more water-resistant and chemical-resistant finish than traditional lacquers. It is however much more difficult to repair so that should be taken into consideration when deciding upon your cabinet finish.

One final note on cabinetry finishes. Most high-end kitchen cabinets are finished in place. What this means is that most of the cabinets you see in modern magazines have been installed *unfinished*. Then all the crown molding, baseboards, and trim work is done. After this, the professional finishers come in and spend weeks filling all the nail holes and damage done by the installation. Finally it's all sanded and final finishing takes place to get that perfect finished look. Because your remodel probably won't have the budget for finished-in-place cabinets, you can expect to see nail holes and some small damage that will need to be repaired in place during installation.

For a more detailed analysis of finishes and the pros and cons of lacquers versus conversion varnish, visit *www.divinekitchen.net/ good-finishes*.

 ## Cabinet Standards

There are a lot of decisions to make when designing a kitchen, but thankfully cabinets are made with standard dimensions. Here's how these dimensions work in a kitchen.

Upper Cabinets

Just like it sounds, these are the wall cabinets that go to the ceiling. The industry standard is to create uppers 12″ deep, though our shop typically makes them a little deeper (13″ –14″) for easier storage of larger plates.

Base Cabinets

All base cabinets are 24″ deep, as this is the industry standard. In our shop, we never diverge from this standard unless it's for an island cabinet. There are several reasons for this. All full-extension drawer slides only fit in a 24″ deep cabinet. If you make the cabinet deeper, the space is wasted because the drawers won't go all the way to the back. In addition, most standard countertops are only 25½″, providing a 1½″ overhang past the cabinets.

Countertops

The enormous variety of materials available has only made it more complicated for the average family to choose a suitable option. I have been a certified fabricator and installer for the past ten years so I have worked with just about everything on the market. Each material has its own particular quirks and unique properties.

The five most frequently chosen options—engineered stone, granite, quartz, marble, and Corian—work well in any kitchen. Remember to make sure that the fabricator you hire has experience working with a range of materials so that he or she isn't learning about a new material while working on your job.

Countertop Depth

The industry standard for most modern countertops is 25½″ deep. This will give you a 1½″ overhang from the cabinets. This overhang is *very* important because it prevents water and food dripping down the front of your cabinets. In the past, tile was often installed with almost no overhang at all, thus creating a huge mess, especially in front of the sink area. **Make sure you have an adequate overhang with your new countertops**.

Template

This refers to the physical template that is made after your new cabinets are installed. We make templates out of strips of thin wood, plastic, and other materials. It is like a dress pattern. It's a full-size exact replica of what your finished countertops will be. In order to make an accurate template, the countertop fabricator will need to have your new appliances in place, including the stove. This is because the template needs to be positioned right next to the stove exactly as the new (heavy) countertops will be positioned.

A good fabricator will usually take an hour to do a complete template. He or she will take into consideration any potential problems, difficult areas for installation, where the field seam will be, sink location, stove and cooktop location, where the finished edge is and any other instructions needed during fabrication. An inexperienced or casual fabricator will skim through it quickly or worse, not do a template and instead do a drawing on a notepad. Without a proper template, you will have a poor installation with multiple problems and delays.

Field Seam

This occurs when, during installation, two pieces of finished countertop are joined together using a color-matched epoxy. Field seams are required because the materials are extremely heavy, they have to change shape, and often cannot be made or transported in one whole piece. A good fabricator takes his time determining the best place to put field seams, trying to minimize their appearance so they don't stand out. You will typically have one or two field seams in your countertops.

Engineered stone is a very consistent thickness and thus is the easiest to create good, tight, and even field seams. Granite often has varying thicknesses that can create difficulty when trying to make a flat, tight field seam. A good fabricator/installer knows how to match color and pattern for a good field seam. The joint(s) should not be noticeable.

Profile

The profile refers to the actual design or shape of the finished countertop edge. This is the finished or pretty edge. The most common profiles are bullnose, half bullnose (sometimes called pencil edge), bevel, round over, ogee (an S shape), large ogee, and square polish. A typical front edge thickness is 1½″. This is because the material is usually ¾″ thick and during fabrication we epoxy a strip of ¾″ material on the front edge, thus creating a 1½″ front countertop edge.

Lamination

This is extremely important! This is the process of cutting a matching strip of granite or engineered stone, and gluing it with a high-quality epoxy to the edge of the finished front of the countertop. It is then routed and polished to create the finished "profile" that you call the front edge of your countertop. A good fabricator will ensure a tight (very small) line *with a matching pattern.* A matching pattern means that the fabricator cut the strip from the same location so that when it is glued on, the pattern will flow through the profile. ***This is the sign of a well-fabricated granite top.*** Typically if this is done correctly, then the rest of the countertops will be fabricated and installed correctly. A poor fabricator may not use the right epoxy color, will not match the pattern, and/or will poorly clamp the seams during fabrication. This leads to a large noticeable joint and a sloppy appearance. It is also a good indication of the rest of the job not being done well; so be wary of this type of fabricator!

Prefabrication vs. Custom Fabrication

There is a huge amount of deception that goes on in this industry. And nothing is more misunderstood than the difference between custom fabrication and prefab installation. This is why it is very important to learn about this aspect of your job.

"Prefab" or prefabricated slabs already have the edge glued on and routed. They come in precut lengths, but the installer will then trim them down to fit your cabinets. He or she will also have to make the sink cutout and various other alterations to make the slab work in your kitchen. The upside is that this is a cheaper way to get granite or engineered stone installed in your house.

The downsides are many. Even buying the exact same color of stone will not guarantee that your field seams will match, often creating a very noticeable difference in color and pattern. This is because prefab slabs come from many different sources and/or are cut from the Earth at different times. So a slab of Madera gold cut today looks different from a slab cut from the same location one month later. They are similar but not the same. The only way to make sure they are the same is to cut both pieces from the exact same slab.

Many lower-quality fabricators use prefab materials but don't tell their customers they are doing it. These deceptive tradespeople are often the least experienced and will cut sink holes poorly, do a shoddy installation of the backsplash, and create a host of other problems. Typically these companies make their money on speed and will often hurry to quickly get through the installation, skipping steps good fabricators and installers would never rush.

Now I'm not saying a good fabricator cannot buy prefab slabs and do a beautiful installation job. It is an alternative if you have limited funds. But generally, the better fabricators are less likely to use prefab slabs because prefab slabs don't allow for good lamination and unobtrusive field seams. Only custom slabs allow them to do that.

Custom fabrication involves buying full-size raw slabs. Each slab should be handpicked by you and your fabricator at the slab yard. Bring your door sample and any other samples that you'll need to complement the granite. (If you bring your idea board you'll have all you need.) In this way you can be in control of the exact color and pattern. Custom fabrication usually takes two weeks; installation just one.

Your fabricator will have those slabs delivered to his shop where he will use the template previously created to cut up those raw slabs. He will then cut strips from matching locations and laminate all the edges to create a countertop out of raw slabs. Finally he will route your profile design and spend many, many hours polishing to create a finished product. This costs more than prefab but the benefits far outweigh the difference in price. Good fabrication and installation takes a true craftsman and is not a job to be taken lightly. You will be looking at it every day, touching it every day, and your selection of the appropriate materials and contractor is a very important decision. Outside of the cabinets and appliances, I feel this is the most important choice to make in your kitchen remodel. Choose wisely.

Picking a Good Countertop Color

If you decide to go with custom fabrication, please take the extra step and visit various slab yards. Slab yards are distributors of wholesale slabs of granite and engineered stone. They allow you to walk around and choose your slabs. Often there will be retail prices posted usually showing the price per square foot. Once you have picked a slab, your fabricator can often negotiate a better price depending on his relationship with that distributor.

Do not leave slab selection up to your fabricator and do not look at just a small sample. You need to look at the full-size slabs and take some time to think about all the various aspects before choosing a color. The abundance of gorgeous options can be truly overwhelming the first time you visit a showroom. Don't worry, and just concentrate on the color palette you have on your storyboard. Do not be distracted by the many, many beautiful choices.

I usually help my clients narrow the selection process by using the following guidelines:

1. Decide if you want a small amount of contrast or a large contrast between your cabinet and the countertop. If you choose a similar color of countertop and cabinet, say light white countertop and white cabinets, then you will notice the entire kitchen when you walk in the room. If you pick a contrasting color of countertop, you will notice the countertops and their shape in the kitchen first. It just depends on what you like most. Some people really like a sharp contrast and some people like to see the overall effect of the kitchen.

2. Be very careful of picking colors like green, blue, pink, or any other color that is *not a neutral*. You will see some amazing granite patterns and colors. Just remember that if you pick a *green* countertop your kitchen will always be green. And women often change their preferences over the years. You may want a bright yellow kitchen today but might want a Tuscany green Italian kitchen in three years.

3. Always bring a sample of your *flooring* with you. Remember that countertops are not seen in a vacuum. You will be standing above it, looking down, past your cabinet color to your floor. It is impossible to not see your floor when looking at your countertop, so make sure you are comfortable with all three in one glance.

4. Overall *darkness and lightness* is important. Try to remember that if you have a small kitchen with inadequate light, picking a black countertop probably isn't the best choice. Spend some time thinking about your specific space, is it adequately lit? How big is it? How much countertop space is there? Try to visualize the color you like taking up the space and what its overall effect will be.

5. Remember the *26" rule*! When looking at a slab that is nine feet long by six feet tall, it can be hard to visualize it as anything but a big gorgeous hunk of stone. So **bring a small measuring tape with you** and visually cut it up into 26" deep strips to mimic what it will look like as finished countertops. Often when you do this, the "pattern" that you thought was so obvious and beautiful would be lost once cut up.

6. Finally, if you find some *particular element*, pattern, or shape that you love in a particular slab, be sure to mark it on the slab when talking with your fabricator. If there is something you want placed in a particular area of your kitchen, be sure to let him know or that "something special" might just get cut out during fabrication.

Engineered Stone

This is a man-made material produced by combining various materials like quartz. It is highly consistent and considered the toughest against heat and cutting. It is nonporous and thus bacteria-resistant. Generally, it has a very consistent pattern and thus does not look like a natural stone. It has a very consistent price because supply and demand is more closely regulated. Examples would be HanStone, Cambria, Zodiak, and Silestone.

Granite

Natural stone is cut from stone quarries around the world. It is very hard but porous compared to engineered stone. Its color, pattern, size, and density varies dramatically from slab to slab. Therefore the range in prices varies significantly and is based on supply and demand. The industry has made a big deal out of sealing it, however many granite slabs come with a very strong seal already applied by the distributor. This material is an extremely durable option, requiring minimal sealing, which is easily done.

Both engineered stone and granite are equally good options to me, considering the way the average family uses their countertops. The only real reason I would choose one over the other is from a design standpoint. Engineered stone has a uniform appearance and a consistent pattern whereas granite can have lots of dynamic and varied elements going through it. It is often referred to as "movement" in the industry. Movement refers to the natural colors or minerals that create a sense of direction or pattern through the granite slab.

To view examples and further discussion about each brand of engineered stone, quartz and granite, visit *www.divinekitchen.net/ good-countertops.*

Marble

This is a natural stone cut from stone quarries around the world. It is very porous and because of that, stains easily. You cannot cut on this product directly without leaving visible scratches. ***It must be sealed properly and maintained***. Not every fabricator is well equipped to work with this product, so be sure to use someone who is familiar with its special qualities. The price for various colors and hard-to-find varieties can range widely and is also based on supply and demand. White Carrara and Calacatta marble is a very popular material. It's shown in popular magazines and widely discussed with both pros and cons. It is *extremely* popular with women and in demand all the time.

Since we fabricate and install it frequently and I have it in my own home I can give you my personal opinion. White Carrara is a soft stone. If you cut on it, you will see your cut lines. I use a wood cutting board, which also saves my knives from getting dull. If you drag heavy, sharp, or ragged items across the surface you will see scratches. So if these types of things bother you than it is not a good option. *It needs a very strong sealer* which should be applied once a year. If you don't seal it you will see all kinds of rings, stains, and marks from every liquid that is placed on its surface. Lemons, water rings, and wine-glass rings will all show up immediately.

This is part of its appeal and is why it's been used in Italy and places around the world for centuries. We call this a "patina" in the industry. After a while, you don't notice the marks and you just enjoy the patina of your beautiful countertop. And there are numerous ways to remove stains and create "poultices" if you decide you want to spruce it up after a few years. The upside is that it's great for baking and rolling out bread and pizza. It is the preferred material for many great chefs and bakers. Martha Stewart has it all over her kitchen.

If you decide that white Carrara marble is for you, be sure to hire a fabricator who has lots of experience fabricating this material specifically. You want someone who can create a profile with a minimal visible joint, knows how to get a good field seam, and who has experience with quality sealers.

For detailed pictures and discussion about the difference between Carrara and Calacatta marble, visit *www.divinekitchen.net/good-marble*.

Corian

This is a synthetic product, man-made from various polyesters. It is nonporous and bacteria-resistant and which is why it is used in hotels, hospitals, and many commercial applications. Corian products are remarkable for their integrated seamless sinks, invisible field seams, and are the only material that can be resurfaced and repaired in case of damage. Corian is less expensive than the previously mentioned products and the price is consistent. You cannot cut directly on the surface or place hot items on Corian countertops, so you will need to be sure that you use a cutting board and pot holders or trivets if you choose this product.

I have fabricated and installed Corian for many years and in many different applications. I love this product and it is a great option for those seeking a beautiful look for less money than granite or engineered stone. It has gotten a bad rap in the industry, but from what I see it is usually because of a poor color selection, poor fabrication, or a bad installation. This is a great option if you pick a good color and it's properly fabricated and installed.

Sinks

There are lots and lots of opinions on sinks, so I will cover the things that come up the most and share what I've learned over the years.

Kitchen sinks typically come in four materials. These include stainless, porcelain, solid surface, and granite composite. Besides picking the material and color, you will need to decide on the type of installation. You will also need to pick a faucet and determine how many attachments you want. The number of attachments dictates how many holes will be drilled through the countertop material behind the sink on the day of your countertop installation.

When you pick out a sink shape remember that if you pick a sink with a straight back, usually a single or evenly split double bowl, then you will have the most space available for faucet attachments. If you pick an unusual shape or an uneven bowl, usually a large bowl and small bowl combo, then your number of faucet attachments will be limited because the holes can only go behind the smaller of the two bowls. We can usually fit four holes behind the smaller sink bowl. In modern kitchen countertops we rarely if ever attach the faucet to the sink anymore. The faucet is almost always attached through the countertop.

Topmount (TM)

This refers to a sink that is installed over the "top" of the countertop. It is installed after the countertops are installed and is typically (though not always) installed by the plumber when he or she hooks up the new water. It has a finished edge all the way around since that is visible. Typically, the countertop fabricator cuts the hole that the sink goes in but does not install or set the sink. After the countertops are installed, the plumber installs the sink, and hooks up the faucet and dishwasher.

Undermount (UM)

This refers to any sink that is installed before the countertops are installed. By installed, I mean set in place in the new cabinet and then the countertop is installed over it. It is therefore mounted "under" the countertop. The responsibility for the fit falls on the shoulders of the countertop installer. Once the countertop installer is finished installing the sink and the countertops, then the plumber hooks up the new water to the sink, but he is not responsible for its placement since its goes underneath the countertop and cannot be moved once the countertops are installed. This type of UM sink gives the tightest joint and ensures minimal bacteria and "eeck" around the sink. It is considered a permanent installation since the counters have to be removed to reinstall a new one.

Farmhouse or Apron (UM)

This type of sink has a front apron that extends past the cabinet front. It has a distinct look but does have some extra cost associated with it. The most popular is made of porcelain and is usually a large single bowl. It is more expensive because you will need a custom cabinet that can support this large heavy sink. It needs to be built specially to be able to support 200 lbs., so it is very difficult to move around. Additionally, the countertop fabricator will charge more for the extra labor and attention that is needed for the precise fit of the sink against the countertop. I would not recommend you choose this style of sink if you have an inexperienced countertop fabricator. A very precise fit is required and often installers have not had much experience performing this technique. Verify before you purchase this sink that you have a fabricator/installer that is very competent with this type of installation.

Stainless Steel

This is still the most popular material in kitchen sinks. It is the least expensive, is an excellent option for cleanup and has many bowl styles and options. You will often find the cheapest brands and lowest quality of steel sold at the big box stores. I've also seen inferior stainless steel sinks sold through fabricators so choose wisely. I would personally never install less than 16 gauge and would prefer to buy it through a reputable dealer. My favorite brand is called Bella (distributed by Affinity Surfaces), which is sold through local fabricators.

Porcelain

It's an old favorite. Many women still prefer porcelain and it will probably never go out of style. Typically porcelain is more expensive than stainless or solid surface. They are more difficult to install because they are heavy. Care should be taken to ensure that the cabinet is built to provide adequate, stable support. Porcelain sinks come in many shapes, colors, and sizes, with Kohler still being the preferred brand. A standard single white bowl is less expensive, while multiple bowels and color options cost a bit more.

Solid Surface

This sink is the only option if you want a truly seamless, integrated look and feel. Solid surface has many bowl shapes and options and they come in a range of neutral colors. This style of sink is made of the same polyester material as the countertop and is in fact "glued" on to the underside of the countertop. After some routing and sanding it becomes part of the countertop with no seam. It is a great option if you want a completely seamless look and feel. The only downside is that you can't drop a hot pan into the sink because it will create a burn mark in the surface. To avoid this, simply add some water to any hot pans first and then set them down in the sink bowl.

Granite Composite

This is the newest material option and there have been many recent improvements to it. A combination of crushed granite and resin, it is very resistant to scratches and dents. However it has its drawbacks as well. In darker colors it tends to show water and mineral deposits unless it is wiped out each day. In lighter colors it tends to stain and must be cleaned regularly. Do your research and make sure you understand the pros and cons of this new style of sink before purchasing. You can see a wide range of detailed reviews at *www. houzz.com*. My preferred brand for this type of sink is Blanco.

Faucet Holes

All holes for faucets and attachments are cut the same, a standard size of 1⅜". Even if it looks like the items are different, in the industry we always cut the same size hole. Remember it is critical to be onsite the day of the countertop installation to determine where and how many holes to drill. It is typically near the end of the installation but not always. Make sure that your countertop fabricator/installer knows that you want to participate in determining the layout. But be warned, it is common for the fabricator to just drill the holes where he "thinks" they should go and this will probably NOT be where you want them as the homeowner.

Air Gap

This little item is a relief valve that is on top of your countertop. Its purpose is to make sure that, should your dishwasher get plugged up, it doesn't back up into your sink. Many modern dishwashers have an internal air gap built into them so that you don't need to put this on the countertop next to your faucet. Check with your plumber to find out if that is the case, otherwise you will need an additional hole next to your faucet to connect this device to your dishwasher.

Air Soft

This cute little device is the modern way to turn your garbage disposal on and off. Instead of using the traditional switch on the wall near your sink, an air soft is a nice little button on your countertop next to your faucet that you push to turn it on and off. It's quite convenient and inexpensive to include. Just make sure your countertop fabricator/installer knows if you need additional hole drilled for this item.

 # Appliances

Researching appliances is fun but exhausting since there are so many options. Even though the market is flooded with numerous brands and lots of varieties, I compiled a list of what is most often installed in typical kitchens. This does not include the numerous specialty brands, like Viking, Wolf, and Sub-Zero. These manufacturers are typically too expensive for most homeowners. If you find you are interested in any of these specialty brands as an option, be sure to research all of the costs associated with installation. They often require special handling, installation, and hookup by certified installers.

Refrigerators

The most common refrigerator is still a standard 36″ wide. They are typically 69–70″ tall. Depths range a lot depending on the square footage. Be sure to measure the depth yourself when planning your kitchen. Take into account how far the refrigerator will stick out into the room (including the door and handles). I usually *strongly* recommend a counter-depth design. This is a model that has a reduced depth to better fit within the space. No matter which style you choose, be sure to measure the depth of the case, the part up to the door, to give to your cabinetmaker if you are installing a refrigerator cabinet. This will ensure that your upper cabinets above the refrigerator are reachable. If the cabinet isn't deep enough to sit almost flush with the refrigerator, these cabinets are worthless.

Also remember that when you position your refrigerator, it needs space to breathe in the back, sides, and top. We typically position them no closer than 1–2" from the back wall.

Counter-Depth Refrigerator

This refers to a refrigerator this is shallower than the older styles we all grew up with. The actual depth varies by brand and maker, so take a tape measure with you to the store to find out for yourself or look at the products' specification pages online. Even if its doors are not flush with the finished depth of the countertop at 25½", counter-depth refrigerators still help to visually reduce the appliance's overall profile, minimizing its chance of physically or visually interfere with the kitchen's flow. Typically we build the cabinet to enclose the "case" or the part of the refrigerator up to the door hinge.

French Door Refrigerator

This refers to a two-door refrigerator with freezer combo on the bottom. It is extremely popular and looks great in most kitchens, but they do come with some constraints. There is significant reduction of space in both the refrigerator and freezer sections. Make sure you will be able to fit all of your food in this style of refrigerator. You will also need to be sure that in your design there will be enough room next to the refrigerator to get both doors fully open. You don't want to bring it home only to discover that you can't take the vegetable drawers out because the refrigerator doors won't open all the way due to the adjacent wall.

Product Reviews

It's nice to know what other consumers think, but be careful about putting too much stock in appliance reviews. Use them to get a general overview about various options but *never use them to actually pick what will work for your family*. In my experience the only clients who are happy with the end result are those who personally went and visited each appliance. They watched the way the door opens, how it binds on the corner, if the veggie drawers pull out without the door being all the way open. Be sure to open all the little doors and drawers, look at how much room you actually get—or don't get. These things are impossible to tell just by looking at the product and the reviews online.

Ordering Online

A word of caution about ordering appliances online. Most appliances, around 60%—yes, really—have to be returned because something is wrong with them. The waterline doesn't work in the refrigerator, not all the burners work on the stove, there are dents, the handle is broken, etc. You name it, I've seen. So purchase your appliances from a local source. Verify their return policy and what they will do in case of damage. Bottom line, it is very difficult to return any appliance purchased online, so be careful.

Appliance Delivery

Most homeowners take for granted appliance delivery and installation. But the hardest part is getting them delivered, in the house and installed with no damage. Be aware that many appliance sellers do not install their appliances and consider delivery to be "in the driveway". It is your responsibility to get them in your house and installed. So before you purchase anything, make sure you have a plan.

Somebody has to be at home to accept delivery, inspect for damage and coordinate getting heavy, awkward appliances safely into your house without damaging the floor or walls. The truth is that most damage to your new floor happens by inexperienced delivery drivers or installers. Make a plan to protect your floors. ***Cardboard and/or paper will NOT be sufficient.*** We use cabinet blankets during installation and ⅛″ Masonite to protect the floor during delivery and installation. Almost every appliance, especially refrigerators and stoves, will leave marks on the floor due to their weight if the flooring is not protected by Masonite or some type of dense hard material.

Freestanding Stove

This stove always has feet, sits on the ground, and typically has a back. It is the most common type of stove or oven. The countertop is fitted next to it within an ⅛″ on each side, but does not go behind the stove, making it the least expensive way to fabricate a countertop and the most common.

Slide-In Stove

In the past this kind of stove did not have feet. Instead of standing on the ground, it rested inside of a custom-built cabinet. It did not have a back and thus the countertop material had to be custom-made to fit behind the stove. Because of this custom fabrication, the labor cost for countertops using this type of stove was higher.

Recently, they have begun making these stoves with feet that rest on the ground, but the countertop material still has to go around the back of the stove. They are still more expensive to install because of the very precise fit required. The extra labor and knowledge to do it correctly will cost more, so you should plan accordingly.

Double Oven

Typically, double ovens are two, stacked wall ovens; one is usually smaller than the other. Prices range from $3,000–$8,000. They typically need a special cabinet built to support the units' weight. There is also usually an extra electrical cost for setup and installation.

Convection Oven

Convection ovens are something in between an oven and a microwave. They cook faster than traditional ovens by circulating air, providing more consistent temperatures throughout the oven and fewer hot spots. While they can cook faster (and more efficiently) than traditional ovens, they don't produce the yucky texture that usually comes with cooking meat in a microwave.

Cooktop

This type of unit sits within the countertop and allows for storage in the base cabinet under the unit. It has elements for cooking, but no oven. It comes in both gas and electric models, and prices range dramatically depending on options.

Downdrafts

This is a fan or vent that is installed behind the stove unit and vents through the floor. They are expensive and need additional gas and electrical work, as well as venting when installing. Homeowners are usually unprepared for the extra costs associated with installing this type of unit. Do not purchase this unless you have talked with your cabinetmaker, countertop fabricator, plumber (if using gas), and electrician to be aware of all the extra costs associated with this kind of unit.

Hood Vent

This can be as simple as a standard 30″ or 36″ hood vent, or as complicated as a special unit that is installed within a custom wood hood. Be sure to talk with your cabinetmaker and electrician to ensure you are aware of the extra costs. Typically, the more expensive the hood vent, the more complex and expensive the installation.

Flooring

Most families install one of three flooring materials during a kitchen remodel. There is a lot of debate within the industry about which flooring material is best in a kitchen. All of these options can work well if installed correctly. Tile has always been the traditional material and is a great option, but engineered wood flooring has come a long way and is commonly installed in modern kitchens to add warmth and softness.

Remember that, in all of these flooring types, the overall pattern will vary. In wood flooring, a well thought out and consistent color throughout the floor is optimal—unless you want a patchy, mismatched color scheme on purpose. Be sure you discuss the layout, pattern, and color variations of your materials with your installer before installation begins. Lastly, **always** install all types of flooring completely underneath your dishwasher, refrigerator and stove. Do not allow the installer to short-cut this step to "save material." This is the number one way that water damage occurs and ruins your new kitchen if there is a leak.

Engineered Wood Flooring

Engineered wood flooring has a hardwood top, typically ⅛" thick, and a plywood substrate. The plywood substrate gives the material much greater stability and resistance to changes in temperature and moisture. With its tongue and groove design, it can be installed as a floating floor, glued down, or nailed down. Floating floors are the noisiest and have a spongy feel. Nailing down the floor will remove the sponginess. Gluing down the floor will be the quietest and feel the softest on your feet. It is a very stable product with minimal wood movement due to the plywood substrate. This is our preferred flooring to install, and we typically use a glue-down installation method when possible.

Hardwood Flooring

This is usually ¾" thick solid hardwood. Installation is typically nail or glue down and varies based on the type of wood species and how much moisture there is in a given location. It is not considered a stable product since it is solid wood and is very susceptible to changes in temperature and moisture. This is because solid wood, especially in large amounts, grows and shrinks depending on its moisture content. It is a beautiful product when properly installed. However, the price is significantly higher and should only be installed by a licensed professional, since steps must be taken to ensure long-term stability.

Tile

There many tile options for your kitchen floor and backsplash. All of them are good options for the kitchen. Always buy an extra box for repairs and damage to tile over the years, because it is very difficult to purchase matching tile several years after the initial purchase.

Electrical

Electrical work is probably the most misunderstood and the least appreciated aspect of a remodel. From a homeowner's point of view, I understand. You've been living with what you have for a long time you're used to the dim lighting and the outlets that shut off. But without adequate lighting your new cabinets and countertops *will not* look like the fancy magazines you've been browsing. You will enjoy your new kitchen more when it is bright and shiny.

In addition, you want to have dedicated circuits for your new appliances. This will ensure that when you plug your toaster in on one side of the room, you don't blow a fuse and turn off your new refrigerator! This is also a great opportunity to upgrade to modern matching outlets, including the new style where you can plug your iPhone directly into a USB outlet. It's not super expensive but it instantly makes your kitchen look new and updated. How nice to be able to get rid of those bulky plugs and simply use the sleek USB cord!

Can Lighting

Also known as recessed lights, can lights are flat and unobtrusive lights installed in ceilings. It has a flush and clean design look. Typically, they create more light (using light-emitting diodes or LEDs) and focus your attention on the beautiful kitchen instead of on a specific light fixture.

Dimmer Compatibility

Some LED lights or fixtures are not dimmer-compatible. Be sure to verify with your electrician that all lights and fixtures, including undercabinet and task lighting, IS dimmer compatible.

Ground Fault Circuit Interrupter (GFCI)

This is a special type of outlet that is required within 6 ft. of water (such as a sink) to protect against fire.

Dedicated Circuits

These are outlets that are only used for one purpose, for example a microwave, refrigerator, dishwasher, stove, oven, or garbage disposal. When you upgrade your kitchen, it is recommended that each of these items should be on a dedicated outlet. In California, it is required but rarely enforced.

Plumbing

One of the most common misconceptions related to plumbing is that the cost of the countertop includes plumbing repair and installation—it does not. Often there is much needed work that only a professional licensed plumber can perform. I've seen customers try to skip this important step or attempt to do the work themselves, often causing damage to their new cabinets.

Supply Valve

These are the valves that supply your faucet and dishwasher with hot and cold water. That's why there are two of them. They are typically rusted and leaking and should be replaced. A professional plumber can easily replace them for a modest fee. Leaving the old leaking ones in place is a sure way to allow water damage to ruin your new cabinets.

Sink Strainer

This is the small circular device that fits into your drain. It is what attaches your sink to the drain and pipes below. Most sinks do not come with sink strainers so you or your plumber must buy them. All garbage disposals come with a strainer but often if you have a double bowl sink you must buy two matching strainers if you want them to be the same.

Garbage Disposal

Unless you have purchased your garbage disposal in the last two to three years, you probably want to upgrade. Modern garbage disposals are very powerful and even the least expensive model is much better than those made twenty years ago. It will come with a strainer but not with a power cord, so plan on buying that separately or your plumber will add it into his bid.

Dishwasher

It is typically less expensive to hookup an existing dishwasher because it already has its power cord and supply line attached. A brand new dishwasher costs more because it doesn't come with those items included and they take time to attach. Keep an eye on your dishwasher for the first few days after installation. This is usually when they leak and may need some slight adjustment.

Quality Control Library

As a homeowner it can be really difficult to judge whether a job is well done or not. Even if you are handy and do a lot of projects yourself, you are probably unaware of professional industry standards.

To help you determine the quality of the job, what follows is what I look for when I'm inspecting a job. These are the qualities you should be looking for within each trade. Obviously it's not exhaustive and isn't meant to substitute for working with high-quality contractors, it's just meant to give you some idea of what are the most important things to notice *before* you make your final payments.

Cabinets

Level: base cabinets should finish at 34½″ from the finished floor, and be level left to right and front to back. The opening where the stove goes, is usually 30″ wide, and should be plumb and parallel.

All doors and drawer fronts should be adjusted to have even reveals and be consistently spaced. All doors and drawers should open and shut easily and have little rubber bumps to protect your cabinet finish.

All filler and scribe moldings should have the tiniest nail holes, which should be filled with *matching* putty.

All shelves should be installed and be adjustable.

All crown molding and baseboards should have unnoticeable holes from nails and be filled with *matching* filler.

Interior: All uppers should be attached with 3″ screws and holes covered with matching fastcaps.

Countertops

All countertops should be level (left to right and front to back). The opening for the stove should be 30″ wide and not expose the plywood underneath.

Countertop edges should be square polished along the edge nearest the stove.

The backsplash (usually 4″–6″ tall) should be lined up evenly with the countertop and not be too long or short.

All profile edges should be polished and smooth.

All field seams should be color matched, pattern matched, and flat with a minimal joint using a matching color epoxy. No field seam in granite will be invisible, but it should be minimized as much as possible.

There should be no glue or silicone or adhesive dripped onto the cabinets during installation.

There should be no scratches or dents on the cabinets or appliances during installation.

There should be a very small, unnoticeable silicone line between the counter-top and backsplash. The color should match very well. A beautiful job can be ruined by a horrible silicone color choice that stands out like a sore thumb.

Around the sink the silicone should be applied in a small even line, without smears all over the new sink.

The countertop should have a consistent 1½″ overhang from the countertops.

The lamination line where the granite is glued together to form the profile (the pretty edge at the front that you look at every day) should be unno-ticeable and the pattern of the granite should flow or match.

 ## Wood Flooring (Engineered and Hardwood)

All doorway casings should be undercut so the wood goes underneath, not around moldings.

There should be no visible raw edges; floors should be even with no high spots or humps. There should be no cracks between boards, no squeaks, and no glue anywhere on the floor.

Seams should never fall within 6″ of each other.

A well-thought out and consistent color throughout the floor is optimal, unless you purposely want an eclectic, busy, patchy, and high-contrast color scheme.

Appliances

Sixty to seventy percent (60% –70%) of appliances are delivered with some kind of defect. Look for problems such as:

- Icemaker doesn't make ice
- Water dispenser doesn't work
- Dents
    + In front of door on refrigerator
    + On handles of refrigerator
    + In front of dishwasher
    + On front door of stove
- Dishwasher leaks
- One or more stove burners won't light or don't work
- Feet bent or broken off of stove or dishwasher during installation
- Lights don't come on in the refrigerator
- Stove won't turn off

These are just the most common ones I see from a variety of manufacturers. I have a current client that has had six deliveries of the same appliance; the fridge has showed up dented each time. How frustrating! So what I try to tell my clients is to expect something to happen and have the floors protected.

 ## Tile

A well-installed tile job should be even and flat, with no high spots or ridges.

I recommend *small* grout lines and an *unnoticeable, well-blended* grout color. Do not assume your installer will pick a good color. Often they spend very little time thinking about the grout color so be involved and specify that you want it to match well.

Tile should be sealed and the sealer wiped off immediately otherwise a haze will form and it can be difficult to remove later depending on the tile you selected.

There should be no chips and tiles should be evenly aligned with well-thought out transitions and moldings.

Plumbing

A well-designed plumbing job under the sink should look clean and use the minimal amount of pipe to hook up the new sink.

All joints should be tight and waterproof. And of course, the cabinets should be free of scratches and dents.

Note: Be careful of plumbers touching your new cabinets and countertops with dirty hands, often creating damage that is irreparable. I always remove the kitchen sink cabinet doors, during plumbing installation and tape rosin paper on the bottom of the sink cabinet to prevent black PVC glue from getting all over it. Plumbers' PVC glue is not removable once dripped onto your cabinets.

Your faucet and all attachments should be firmly attached and evenly spaced. They should not be dripping or leaking.

The inside of the new sink should be clean and free of plumbers putty, which is commonly used to seal the sink strainers.

A well-installed refrigerator should be level and the waterline hooked to the back shouldn't leak. Verify this *before* you roll the refrigerator inside the cabinet.

The dishwasher should be level and *tested* by running it through a full cycle.

If you are installing a gas stove or cooktop, your plumber will be the person hooking it up and testing the line for leaking gas.

Make sure all the burners light and turn off, and the oven heats and shuts off.

Electrical

All your outlets should be straight and level with each other, typically all the same height from the countertop.

The outlet boxes should be flush with the sheetrock, not set too deep, angled, or sticking out too far.

Sheetrock

Quality sheetrock repair, texture, or plastering is a truly fine art. Not all sheetrock guys are equal and in order to get the correct affect, it must look original with no discernible repairs. Remember to ask to see examples of their work or ask specific questions of their references to ensure that they can create an original look.

Sheet rock repair should blend in seamlessly with existing texture of walls. Especially on ceilings and in cases of major damage and repair it is even more important.

Do not accept the job if you can see the repair after it's painted.

Acknowledgments

To my husband who has always allowed me to be exactly who I want to be, both tough and tender. It is upon his strong shoulders that I stand tall and reach for the stars. I can't imagine a better person with whom to spend this journey.

To my mom, who has seen it all and loved everything I ever created. Her wholehearted and enthusiastic support was always a true north I could count on and her compassion a tender place I could fall when things got tough.

To my step-daddy, Big Al, you've been a mentor and friend, a compassionate ear and rock-steady advice giver. You taught me what it means to be a leader and the true meaning of fatherhood and family. Your wisdom is something I strive for every day.

To my sister and brother-in-law (who is like a brother), thanks for your continued support through all the trial and errors of my self-employment. You've been there since the "very beginning" and know just how long the journey has been. It is a source of great comfort knowing you guys always have my back.

To Crystal and the BookSparks staff, thanks for the guidance, creative help, and enthusiasm. It is much appreciated. Your calm direction and experience have brought my dreams to light.

To my girlfriends, both new and old who have always been there for a kind word, a spare glass of chardonnay, or a kick in the butt. I truly value all my friendships and a special thanks to JK, MT, and CM. You girls have gotten me through.

A special thanks to all my clients, you have been a big part of my journey. I value your support and trust in me. It has been an honor to work in your homes, and be around your families. Your appreciation of my creativity and hard work has brought me much joy and pride, and it is with a huge thank you that I express just what each job has meant to me.

Last, but not least, to my daddy, who was the first to show his faith in me and prepare me for my journey. His willingness to take risks and push outside comfort zones was instrumental in my education. Whether intentional or not, he showed me, not with words but by actions, that he believed in me and thought I could do anything.

About the Author

Carpentry is in Camille Finan's blood. After growing up on construction sites in the foothills of Northern California and working in her father's shop, the lure of the "American Dream" called her to college. Camille earned an MBA from California State University, Hayward and ran several successful businesses for many years. However, seeking the deep satisfaction of her early days, Camille left "traditional work" and rediscovered her carpentry roots. After working in the carpenters union and eventually getting her contractors license, she found her niche in kitchens and began to notice an alarming trend: the market was severely underserving its female clientele. She turned her back on traditional kitchen design and developed a new system called DFIO (design from the inside out) to solve the most common kitchen problems average families encounter. She has worked with thousands of women to design and build the kitchens of their dreams. She believes in empowerment for women in the construction trades and in 2011, founded CarpentryU, a series of educational workshops designed to teach women to get the most from their power tools.

Notes

CPSIA information can be obtained at www.ICGtesting.com
Printed in the USA
LVOW03s2000011015

456529LV00012B/373/P